What to Name Your Dog

by Carrie Shook

Illustrated by Michael Senett

Second Edition

HOWELL
BOOK HOUSE
New York

To the memory of Bobbie Shook, with love

Howell Book House
Macmillan General Reference
A Simon & Schuster Macmillan Company
1633 Broadway
New York, NY 10019-6785

Library of Congress Cataloging-in-Publication Data

Shook, Carrie.

   What to name your dog/by Carrie Shook; illustrated by Michael
Senett.—2nd ed.
   p. cm.
   Summary: Features a wide variety of potential names and their
sources for your pet dog.

   1. Dogs—Names. 2. Dogs—Anecdotes. [1. Dogs—Names.]
I. Title.
SF422.3.S48   1989   929.9'7—dc19   88-28419
ISBN 0-87605-807-1

15 14 13 12 11 10 9 8

Printed in the United States of America

Contents

If you pick up a starving dog and make him prosperous, he will not bite you. This is the principal difference between a dog and a man.
— Mark Twain

Acknowledgments

WE are very grateful to our editor, Warren Cox, whose assistance was invaluable. We also thank the following people who made contributions to this book: Fran Bodden, Buddy Brooks, Jon Case, Laura Cass, Lisa Cummings, Lindsay Glickman, Anne Johnson, John Langdon, Mary Liff, Bruce Meyer, Nancy Meyer, Michael Shook, R.J. Shook, Robert L. Shook, Lis Smith, Annie Bell Taylor and Karl Weckel.

Introduction

CHOOSING a name for your dog isn't always easy. In fact, it can be harder than naming a child. With kids, you are limited to established human names. Moreover, in a pinch, you can always give a son your name and add Junior, or name a daughter after her grandmother. In naming your dog, however, you face thousands of possible names *and* words.

For example, you can name your dog after your favorite food (Strudel, Tangerine, Yogurt) or after a hero out of history or literature (Napoleon, Shakespeare, Gulliver). You might prefer a name that is related to your occupation (i.e.: Surgeon—Stitches, Clergyman—Miracle, Photographer—"Cheese," Professor—Egghead). If none of these turns you on, you can search out names and words from other languages, like the Yiddish word *ganev* (thief or crook). Or you can narrow down your choices to the country where your dog's breed originated.

You can also use the name of some well-known personality, *or* of that person's dog.

To help you out, we have included a chapter on celebrities' dogs and how their names were chosen. Alternatively, you can choose the name of a canine who is a celebrity in his own right. Even the most famous, like Lassie and Snoopy, are possibilities, although you won't be able to register their names with the American Kennel Club, since, as Chapter Two explains, some very common names are "used up" and no longer available. But don't fret—it's impossible to run out of choices, especially now that you have *What to Name Your Dog* on hand.

We urge you, however, to think very carefully about the name you finally choose, since it will make a difference to you *and your dog*. Use your imagination. And enjoy the process. Naming your dog is only the first of many pleasures you will enjoy with your new pet.

". . . Now let me tell you guys about *my* day at the office. Charlie, you especially are gonna just flip. Well, my new boss, Mr. Hornsby . . . No, no, Chi-Chi, Fawcett was my old boss. Anyway, he comes to me . . . Are you paying attention, Crackers? So, Hornsby walks into my office . . . Now, here comes the good part, Puddles. This is gonna just kill ya . . ."

1

What's in a Name?

"WHAT'S in a name? That which we call a rose by any other name would smell as sweet." Shakespeare's famous line was obviously not written about man's best friend, the dog. Moreover, the statement may not be true. While the young lovers Romeo and Juliet regarded names as merely a hindrance, many a dog becomes deeply attached to his name.

Perhaps this is not so odd. We all find part of our identity in our names. At the very least we have preferences—sometimes very strong ones—about what we are called. Just as you may despise being called by some childhood name like "Shorty," "Tubs" or "Toothpick," your dog may react with equal sensitivity to name-calling. Moreover, you will find that he becomes at least as attached to his own name as you are to yours. To give an obvious example, if you have trained your dog to respond to his name when called, and then call him by another name, he is unlikely to come—unless perhaps it's mealtime.

Canine literature is full of stories of what happens to dogs whose names are changed for one reason or another. The following short story, for example, is based on a true incident.

Kravinski

Sunday was the worst day of the week for Ivan Kravinski. A Russian immigrant, he worked as a busboy six days a week in a restaurant in

7

downtown Boston, and attended night school four nights. His two free evenings he studied in the library, avoiding his empty, dingy apartment. But Sunday was the sabbath: no work, no study. He sat in the little park near his apartment alone, watching families picnic on the grass.

When he arrived in America the year before, in 1918, Ivan spoke no English at all. Even now, his Russian accent was strong and unmistakable. He tried to accept the fact that people avoided him because of that; America was gripped in one of its periodic Red scares, and he was regarded as a Communist. So far—because of his origins, and perhaps because of his shyness—he had made no friends in the new land.

As he sat glumly on the bench, he felt a tugging on his pants leg, and looked down to see a scruffy black-and-tan dog gently pulling on his cuff. It was a little thing, low to the ground, long-haired, and obviously asking for attention.

"Well, hello there," Ivan said, realizing that a dog, at least, would have nothing against his accent. The dog wagged its tail. Tentatively, Ivan reached down to pat it; the dog wriggled under his hand, and then barked one short, happy bark, looking up at him with bright brown eyes.

Ivan patted the dog for a long time, and then pulled up and looked around—whose dog was it? When he got up to leave, the dog followed him. Forced by his conscience, Ivan approached strangers nearby, asking in his thick accent, "Your dog?" Everyone said, "No." Some patted the dog, and one woman said it was beautiful—although in reality its fur was dull and matted, and Ivan could see how thin its haunches were.

"Come on, boy," he said to the dog at last. "You're coming home with me." The dog trotted behind him.

At the apartment, the dog ate and drank so greedily that Ivan took the dishes away for a while, afraid it would get ill. The dog accepted this gracefully and sat at Ivan's feet, his tail thumping against the ragged carpet. Then he got up and explored the living room, sniffing everything.

"No one here but me," Ivan told the dog. "No family. You're it." Suddenly that settled the question he had been mulling over—what to name the little dog? "My name's Ivan Kravinski," Ivan told the dog. "You're family, my brother, so your name is Kravinski too." The dog gave one happy yelp, and Ivan devoted himself to explaining that one must not bark, because the landlady would object. Of course, Kravinski could not understand—yet from that time on, he never barked in the apartment except that one short happy yelp when Ivan felt especially good.

When Ivan came home at night, however, Kravinski could hardly contain his joy. He had to be petted and talked to for at least fifteen minutes, and Ivan was glad to oblige. "Kravinski, I'm very glad to see you too. It is wonderful to come home to a friend. A brother."

The next week, Ivan's grades improved, and the following week too, even though he was spending less time studying now. He was racing through his assignments with total concentration, in order to play with Kravinski. He finished the semester with high honors.

"What's come over you?" the owner of the restaurant asked him one day, as they were closing up.

"What do you mean?" Ivan asked.

"You were so quiet and withdrawn when you came here. Now I see you smiling even at Bennington. Even Bennington!"

"He's not so bad," Ivan said. "He's got a lot of responsibilities running that department store." The owner studied him and said, "Tell you what, Kravinski. I like your attitude. How would you like to become a waiter?"

Ivan's broad smile was answer enough.

Maybe it was because his English had improved so much, he thought six months later—but life had changed incredibly fast. Here he was, moving to a new apartment, this one right on the park, and more than able to afford it with his new job and the good tips he got. He put down a box of pans and looked at Kravinski, who was cavorting at his feet. "New place, Kravinski," he said to the dog. "Maybe thanks to you, brother. Thanks to you!" Kravinski gave one short, happy yelp.

Then life moved on, still faster. Within the year Ivan earned his American citizenship, and the restaurant's customers and waiters gave him a party with a cake. He took a piece home to Kravinski, who dived in with such enthusiasm that he got white icing on his whiskers, eyebrows and ears. Ivan, who had had a little whiskey in his coffee, felt overwhelmed by sentiment. "Enjoy it, boy," he said. "You did it for me." Perhaps that was foolish, he thought; yet he wondered how he ever got through the nights back then without Kravinski solid and warm at the foot of the bed.

Scarcely had Ivan adjusted to being a United States citizen with friends who liked him than one day Mr. Bennington pulled him aside at his table. "You've been waiting on me a long time now," Bennington said, "and I've been watching you work. You're a fine worker." Ivan flushed. "I can't find people like you to work in my store," Bennington went on. "You're cheerful, you're friendly—even to an old curmudgeon like me—you work hard. What're you making?" Ivan told him.

"I'll double it," Bennington said, and the next thing Ivan knew, he had accepted a job as department store clerk.

Bennington, it seemed, had a soft spot for Ivan—or perhaps Ivan really *was* an excellent furniture salesman. In any case, within six months he was manager of the entire department. The day he got that promotion, he couldn't wait to tell Kravinski. "You did it too, boy. We're family. You were my friend, my brother, when I had nobody." Kravinski gave a yelp of joy.

There was only one small shadow on the promotion: Mr. Bennington's suggestion the next day that Ivan change his name. "You're a citizen now," Bennington said, "you have a fine career ahead of you in this store. Now, I'm not telling you anything you don't know, but some people don't like Russian names. It's going to hold you back."

What's in a name? Ivan wondered. The twinge he felt in his stomach was unreasonable. He had found a new and better life here—why not go the whole way and change his name?

"It's the customers," Bennington said gruffly. "Some of them are, ah, somewhat troubled by the idea of a Russian . . . I thought a name like, say, *Kriswell*. Keep the first initial that way, but it's a little more, well, American."

"Kriswell."

"And," said Bennington, "you don't have to make up your mind right now, of course. Really called you in here to tell you you'll be getting five dollars a week more now that you're manager. Forgot to tell you yesterday."

Five dollars a week more! Kravinski was stunned. "Thank you," he said, with sincere gratitude. "And Mr. Bennington . . . I'm going to do it. From now on, call me Ivan Kriswell."

Somewhat to his relief, Ivan found that changing his name did not bother him. For some reason, he was slower to change Kravinski's name—it just didn't occur to him until the day he mentioned the dog to his assistant manager, who said, "He's still got your old name!"

"Why, that's so," Ivan said. That night he went home and sat in his accustomed chair, Kravinski happily on his lap.

"Well, friend," he said, scratching his dog's big pointed ears, "we've come a long way together. You were my first friend in this land, and my best. You are my brother. I am pleased to tell you I have changed our family name. From now on your name is Kriswell, Kris for short, so we are still brothers." The dog did not bark.

The new job was wonderful. Ivan plunged into the intricacies of bookkeeping and faced the challenge of managing his clerks. He had never done work that was so satisfying to him. Oddly enough, he now enjoyed going to the store more than going home at night. There was something wrong at home. Kris felt it too, and no longer greeted him at the door, but lay at the foot of the bed, his pointed snout down on his paws. Nor would he come when Ivan called, "Kris, Kriswell, come here, Kris!"

More worrisome was the fact that the dog would hardly eat.

"Kris," Ivan said, holding the limp animal on his lap, "What's

10

wrong with you?"

The dog just lay there, eyes half shut.

Finally Ivan took him to the veterinarian, who confirmed that the dog was much too thin and listless. "He won't eat," Ivan said, "he doesn't want to play anymore, he doesn't come when I call him. What's wrong with him?"

The vet examined the dog thoroughly. "I'm sorry," he said finally. "I wish I had an answer. I don't know what's wrong with this dog—besides undernourishment. Sometimes they get this way from grief." He shrugged and gave Ivan some tonic to trickle down Kris's throat. Halfway home, Kris simply stopped following Ivan, and stood forlornly on the sidewalk. Ivan carried him the rest of the way.

The next day, Mr. Bennington called Ivan in and read him out unmercifully for an error in bookkeeping that really was unforgivable. Ivan stood and took it, his mind on Kriswell. When he realized Bennington had stopped, he looked up.

"Okay, Ivan," Bennington said in a softer tone. "I don't take back a word I said, understand?" Ivan nodded. "But what's wrong with you? This is not like you."

"My dog," Ivan said simply. "He's very ill. I think . . ." He could not go on. He had intended to say, "I think he's dying."

"Oh," said Bennington with relief. "Well, I can understand that. Man's best friend and all. But don't let it affect your career. You can always get another dog."

Ivan went home that night with despair in his heart. Kris was declining rapidly day by day. That very morning he had actually made a feeble attempt to snap at the master who was once the most important thing in the world to him.

The dog was not at the door, and not on the foot of the bed when Ivan came in. Calling, "Kris, Kris," Ivan went through the apartment. He found the dog curled in the cardboard box the groceries had come in the day before, looking small as a puppy, and showing no signs of life.

"Oh God, don't be dead," Ivan said, reaching out to touch the small bundle, afraid it would be cold and lifeless. Panicking, he cried out, "Kravinski, Kravinski, don't die on me!"

The dog's head came up, and Ivan gasped with relief. "Kris, you furry devil," he cried, taking the dog in his arms. "What's wrong with you? What is it?"

The dog slumped his snout on Ivan's forearm. "Kravinski!" Ivan shouted in despair. And, amazingly, the little black-and-tan face came up, the big brown eyes looked in his, and the dog came out with a short, happy yelp.

Now Ivan knew. He, Ivan, might adjust to a change of identity, but this poor friend could not. He hated to do it, but he had to check. "Kris," he said. "Kris." The dog's head drooped again, and it struggled a little to get out of Ivan's arms.

"All right," Ivan said. "Kravinski! Kravinski! Is that what you want, brother? You want your name back? I'll call you Kravinski then, if that's what it takes to make you eat, foolish brother. Is that what it takes, Kravinski?"

It was. That night, after the two friends had eaten a hearty supper, Ivan fell asleep, a warm, solid lump of dog at his feet, thinking of tomorrow. Tomorrow he would spend with Kravinski in the park, with sunshine and good food and play. It was very fortunate, he thought, that tomorrow was Sunday, the best day of the week.

Kravinski reacted so strongly to the change of his name that only Ivan's love for his dog led him to the solution. The story might well have ended tragically.

In a lighter vein, here is another story which demonstrates that changing a dog's name can be, well, not such a good idea.

A Dog Named Salesman

A New York sales executive and his buddies took a hunting trip to Kentucky. The owner of the lodge assigned each man a bird dog—and the executive got a young, frisky hound, a dog named Salesman.

At the end of the day, the executive was the only one to come back with a full quota of birds.

"Good hunting!" said the lodge owner.

"No, I can't take the credit," the executive replied. "It's Salesman. That is one fantastic dog."

"Yep," said the other man. "Everyone seems pretty happy with him. That's two dollars."

"Two dollars to use that dog all day? That's fantastic." Happily, the executive paid up. And, naturally, he told everyone back home about the lodge in the Kentucky hills, and the super bird dog named Salesman. Some of his friends went down there and came back just as pleased.

The next fall when the executive returned to the lodge, the first thing he did was tell the owner, "I want to reserve Salesman for the weekend."

"Yup," said the owner. "Gotta tell you, though, he's ten dollars a day now."

"Ten!"

The owner shrugged. "He just keeps getting better. Everybody comes down here wants him."

"Well, it's high. But he's worth it, if he's as good as last year."

The dog was even better than the year before, and was obviously the star of the pack, flushing out birds the other dogs didn't detect, and retrieving them from the underbrush without disturbing a feather.

"Here you are," the executive said at the end of the weekend, signing his credit card slip. "Ten bucks a day, and worth every penny of it. That's the best damn bird dog I ever saw."

The next year, he was almost sorry he had talked up Salesman to so many friends. When he returned, the owner informed him, "You can have that dog for the weekend, but he's fifty bucks a day now."

"Fifty!" The executive was aghast.

"Take it or leave it. I got another party coming in that's going to want him. They wrote the dog up in a hunting magazine, you know. Best bird dog in the state, probably the country. He's worth fifty a day."

The man signed. "He probably is. Okay."

Again, his experience with the dog was fabulous. He couldn't wait to get back to the lodge with his full quota of pheasants and rave about Salesman's perfect work.

"Listen," he told the lodge owner. "That dog's too good to be called Salesman. He's the leader of the pack. You ought to rename him Sales Manager."

Pleased with his joke, he picked up his gear and headed for the little airstrip where his plane waited. By now, he decided, the escalation of the dog's worth was becoming rather amusing. Once again he talked up Salesman to people he knew, all the while wondering what the dog would be worth the following year.

He was in for a rude surprise. The next autumn when he returned to the lodge and asked for Salesman, the owner cast an unreadable look at him and said, "You want that hound, you can have him for fifty cents a day."

"Fifty *cents!* Last year he was fifty *dollars.*"

"Yep."

"What happened?"

"Well, if I recollect rightly, you're the fellow gave me the bright idea to give that worthless good-for-nothin' hound a new name."

"Wait a minute, I was just joking."

"Yep. Can't blame you. I thought it was a cute idea. What a mistake! From the minute I told that dog his name was Sales Manager, he ain't done a damn thing but sit around on his backside and howl at the other dogs!"

(Robert Shook, the author's father, has told the above story at sales executive seminars many, many times—always adding that he, too, was once a sales manager.)

There's a moral to both these stories: take care in naming your dog, because this is likely to be the name he carries for life—at his own insistence. One couple we know named their dog after a politician who became national news two years later when he was involved in a major scandal. Blissfully unaware of politics, their dog simply refused to respond to any other name. To this day they apologize for the dog's name to everyone who comes to the house. Cute names—like calling a German Shepherd puppy Littleguy—can be equally tiresome, since most jokes grow old in time.

Whatever name you are attracted to for your dog, ask yourself three questions: Do I really want to call that name in the neighborhood? Am I going to squirm at using the name ten years from now? What am I telling the dog about himself? (He may well pick up the attitude behind a name like Stupid.) Whatever you choose, stick with it. You certainly don't want to turn a frisky, eager Salesman into a howling Sales Manager.

2

American Kennel Club Rules and Regulations for Naming Your Purebred Dog

IF your dog is a purebred, from among the 130 breeds currently recognized by the American Kennel Club and is from a registered litter, you can register it by mail. The AKC, headquartered at 51 Madison Avenue, New York, N.Y. 10010, is a nonprofit organization devoted to the advancement of purebred dogs. As well as registering dogs, the AKC adopts and enforces regulations governing dog shows, obedience trials and field trials, and works to foster the health and welfare of purebred dogs.

Between 1884, when the AKC began registering purebreds, and January 1, 1981, the organization has accumulated the records of over twenty-six million dogs. The growing interest in purebreds is indicated by the fact that since 1970 the AKC has registered about one million dogs each year in its gigantic filing system, known as the Stud Book.

While the AKC registers dogs, owners have the right to name their dogs—within limits. When you bought your purebred, you should have been given an individual registration application; fill out and return this form to AKC, being sure to enter both your first and second choices for the dog's name. The required fee indicated on the form must accompany the application.

There are several restrictions on choice of name. You are not permitted to use Arabic or Roman numerals in your choice, although the AKC reserves the right to assign a Roman numeral in cases of duplication; written numbers are acceptable. The name can contain no more than twenty-five letters—however, the longer it is, within this limit, the more likely it is that nobody else has used it. Any words or abbreviations which imply that the dog has earned an AKC title, such as Champ or Winner, are also no-nos. So are obscenities, degrading names, and words in any alphabet other than English. Also forbidden are: Dog, Male Sire, Bitch, Female, Dam and Kennel.

The name you choose for your dog can have more than one word in it. One convenient way to lengthen the name and make it unique is to add your own surname, as in "Cunningham's Sugar." Make every attempt to come up with two unusual names you like, since very often it is the second name which is accepted. It is also possible that the AKC may send back a Registration Screening Rejection Form explaining why *both* names have been turned down. In that case, you can fill in two more names on the Rejection Form and try again.

There is no assurance that even your second effort will result in an official listing for your purebred—but the AKC does try to help. The organization permits thirty-seven dogs within each breed to be assigned the same name. Even so, many common names, like Spot, Snoopy, Pierre, Lassie, etc. are fully allotted. In some cases, the AKC will accept the name of your choice, but assign it a Roman numeral to differentiate it from other dogs of the same name.

When you fill out the names on the form, be careful to spell and punctuate them correctly; the AKC approves acceptable names exactly as they appear on the application, and will not correct your spelling. If you do misspell the name and discover this fact after the dog is registered, you will not be allowed to correct the error, since this is considered a change in name.

If these procedures seem terribly forbidding, remember that whatever name the AKC accepts for your dog does not have to be his "call name"—the name he responds to. So if all your life you've wanted a dog named Spot, and you end up with an AKC-registered hound named Cunningham's Sugar, take heart—nobody will stop you from calling your dog Spot, and he is unlikely to complain.

3

Dogs in the White House

"THE country at large takes a natural interest in the President's dogs and judges him by the taste and discrimination he shows in his selection . . . Any man who does not like dogs and want them about does not deserve to be in the White House." This statement appeared in the *American Kennel Gazette* in 1924—and in the sixty years since then most American Presidents have demonstrated that they believe it.

While dogs make an impression on the voting public, they have undoubtedly also been a comfort to their White House master. Charlie, John F. Kennedy's Welsh Terrier, may have saved the day for his master during the Cuban Missile Crisis. Tension mounted for Kennedy when it was reported that a Russian fleet might be headed for Cuba to challenge the American blockade. Then the young President asked that Charlie be brought to the Oval Office. He sat stroking the little dog for several minutes, and then returned to the pending crisis.

In a different way, Richard Nixon's political career may have been saved by a dog. When he was vice-presidential candidate in 1952, Nixon was accused of accepting under-the-table gifts. During a famous radio broadcast he declared that the only gift he ever accepted after his nomination was "a little Cocker Spaniel . . . black and white, spotted, and our little girl, Tricia, the six-year-old, named it Checkers." The broadcast went down in history as The Checkers Speech, and is believed to have salvaged Nixon's political career at the time.

17

Franklin D. Roosevelt's Scottish Terrier, Fala, also played a significant role in his political career. Fala was well known to the American public, since Roosevelt often took the dog with him to international conferences for comic relief. But in 1944, Republican politicians accused Roosevelt of sending a destroyer to the Aleutian Islands—at great expense to the taxpayers—to retrieve Fala, who had been accidentally left behind. In a brilliant tactical maneuver, Roosevelt turned the accusation to his advantage during one of his dinner speeches. With unmistakable sarcasm in his voice, the President said: "These Republican leaders have not been content with attacks on me, or my wife, or on my sons. No, not content with that, they now include my little dog, Fala. Well, of course, I don't resent attacks . . . but Fala does resent them . . . I think I have a right to resent, to object to libelous statements about my dog."

Lyndon Johnson lost some supporters through his relationship with his Beagles, Him and Her, when he was photographed picking one of them up by the ears. Dog fanciers were outraged, and Johnson in turn was upset by their failure to understand a good old "Texas Beagle-lifting technique," as he called it.

Despite his roughness with his hounds, there was no doubt that LBJ loved them. When he was still Vice-President, one of his dogs, Old Beagle, died. Johnson had the dog cremated, but couldn't bear to part with the ashes, and kept them in a box over the refrigerator. Finally, the family cook found out what was in that box and blew her top. LBJ consented to have Old Beagle's ashes put to rest at last, in a corner of the family burial plot at the ranch.

Johnson loved unusual gifts, and once accepted a Collie named Blanco from a little girl in Illinois. The gift was irresistible to one who loved animals as much as he did, but immediately presented a problem, since people all over the country began offering or sending similar four-footed gifts. Johnson was forced to announce that his white Collie would have to be symbolic of all the wonderful dogs Americans everywhere had offered him—and that all other dogs would be returned to their senders.

He did not, however, return the dog his daughter Luci gave him while he was still in the White House. The President and Yuki, a little mutt, became inseparable, and it was Yuki who was with him when he died.

Dog-owning Presidents have often displayed a capacity for being just as fond of their dogs as anyone else—and sometimes just as foolish. President Warren Harding was rumored to show more affection for his Airedale, Laddie Boy, than for his wife, with whom he often feuded. Laddie Boy had his own social calendar, and his own chair to sit on at cabinet meetings, which he attended. One year the dog's birthday was

. . . Only Harry Truman got through his term without the comfort of a dog . . .

marked by a party to which the neighborhood dogs were invited. It featured a birthday cake made of dog biscuits topped with icing.

Many White House dogs have been gifts; the most famous of these was undoubtedly Pushinka, offspring of Strelka, the Russian space dog. Pushinka was a gift to John F. Kennedy from Premier Khrushchev. Worried that the dog might have an electronic bug planted in her, the Secret Service examined the new addition to the White House thoroughly. Pushinka was not a spy, however, and became a part of the White House menagerie, which was sizable, since the Kennedys liked animals. Pushinka also contributed to the household a litter of "pupniks" named Blackie, Butterfly, White Tip and Streaker. Later, the President's father, Joseph Kennedy, presented Jackie with a German Shepherd called Clipper; and the Prime Minister of Ireland added a Cocker Spaniel, Shannon. Perhaps because the Kennedys accepted and enjoyed these dogs, a Dublin Priest gave them yet another, an Irish Wolfhound named Wolf. With all the dogs in his household—many of them exotic and beautiful—the President's favorite was always the little Welsh Terrier, Charlie.

Kennedy had no "dog scandals" during his White House days, but Nixon did. His Irish Setter, King Timahoe, was not a well-behaved dog, but the President was very fond of "Tim." Since the dog got airsick flying in the presidential helicopter to Camp David, Nixon had him taken by official limousine. Needless to say, there was criticism when this fact became public. Tim's unruly behavior was not publicized, but it throws some light on Nixon's soft-heartedness. Once when Henry Kissinger was in conference with the President, he noted that Tim had methodically chewed up a sizable strip of rug; Nixon's reaction was to throw the dog some biscuits to divert him. Realizing that Tim naturally thought he had been rewarded, Kissinger teased, "Mr. President, I see you are teaching your dog to chew the rug."

While in office, Nixon owned two other dogs, a Yorkshire Terrier named Pasha, and a Poodle named Vicky. It is not reported whether or not they chewed rugs.

Dwight Eisenhower's Weimaraner, with the pleasant name of Heidi, was extremely camera-shy. She detested Spunky, the little Scottie that belonged to Ike's grandson, David. Nevertheless, since David was the apple of his grandparents' eyes, he was always allowed to bring the Scottie with him, and the two dogs were carefully watched.

Calvin Coolidge was another President with a problem dog. Peter Pan, his Terrier, harassed White House employees so badly that he eventually had to be removed from the White House. Peter Pan was not as fearsome, however, as Franklin Roosevelt's German Shepherd, Major. That dog once put his mark on international relations by biting British Prime Minister Ramsay MacDonald.

20

. . . Kennedy, on the other hand, had nine dogs.

At the other extreme was Liberty, Gerald Ford's Golden Retriever. Far from vicious, Liberty enjoyed a reputation rather similar to that of her master, who was often said to be good-natured but inept. Like many Golden Retrievers, Liberty was overly friendly. She was also slow to respond to obedience training, and had to be enrolled for remedial instruction.

In many cases, we have no way of knowing whether a President named his dog, or whether the donor or a member of the family named it. Often, however, the name and type of dog seem to exemplify something about the man in office. (There were those who always thought it a little suspicious that Harry Truman had no dog at all.) Jimmy Carter had only one dog during his White House days, a mutt given to Amy by her teacher. The mixed-breed dog, with the fine Southern name of Grits, seemed to exemplify the American dream, rising from humble origins to occupy the White House.

Ronald Reagan had a Bouvier des Flandres on Pennsylvania Avenue named Lucky, but the constraints of official life proved too stressful and the dog went to the Reagan ranch in Santa Barbara, California. His place was taken by a Cavalier King Charles Spaniel.

Some people believe that a child who is given the name of a great historical figure will aspire to be like that person. Therefore, if you have high ambitions for your dog and want it to be in training for the White House, you might consider naming it after a President's dog.

4

Trademark Dogs

WHILE many animals have been used as symbols of products, dogs score the highest marks, both in longevity and performance. With his reputation as man's best friend, faithful Fido is a natural salesperson. Depending on his breed, the dog is considered loyal, brave, resolute, pugnacious, ever-obedient, dependable, alert, lovable and fast—to name just a few of his sterling qualities. Small wonder that throughout history dogs have agreed to lend their support to establishments of every kind, by appearing on ancient tavern signboards, knights' crests, business letterheads and in corporate advertising.

In the last category, the most famous dog is undoubtedly RCA's trademark, Nipper, who has been depicted listening intently to "His Master's Voice," as it emanates from a gramophone, for over eighty years. Nipper was modeled on a real black-and-white Fox Terrier born in or near Bristol, England, in 1884. He came to fame only because his first owner died; the owner's brother, Francis Barraud, took the dog with him to his art studio in London.

There Nipper cannily displayed his talents as an artist's model by sitting one day in front of Barraud's gramophone, head cocked, listening to the sounds that came from the large horn. Inspired by this charming pose, Barraud grabbed his brush and palette and painted the scene, which he titled "His Master's Voice." Several attempts to sell the painting were unsuccessful; undaunted, Barraud painted over the black horn of the machine, and transformed it into a brass horn. With this

"His Master's Voice"—This famous painting by Francis Barraud made during the late 1890's gave birth to one of the world's most famous trademarks. In 1929, RCA acquired the Victor Talking Machine Company and American rights to the Dog and Phonograph trademark. On October 31, 1978, RCA launched a new program designed to rejuvenate the trademark.

Famous RCA Trademark Rejuvenated—Here is one version of the famous Dog and Phonograph trademark as it is used in TV and print advertising as an adjunct to the bold contemporary "RCA" letters. The "Nipper" trademark is also used on RCA products, shipping cartons, sales promotion literature and company vehicles.

change, an executive of the Gramophone company liked the painting, but asked Barraud to replace the cylinder machine with a newer disc phonograph. Barraud obliged; Gramophone then bought the oil painting for fifty pounds sterling, and the copyright for another fifty pounds. This was real money for an artist in those days; moreover, the painting made such a hit that Barraud was kept busy the rest of his life making oil and watercolor copies of the original for the company.

In 1901, Nipper at the phonograph became the trademark of the Victor Talking Machine Company. Since then, the trademark has appeared on billions of phonograph records made by Victor and RCA (which acquired the Victor Talking Machine Company in 1921). Nipper's likeness has also been displayed on countless other products, ranging from "Victrolas" to RCA radios and television sets, and has appeared in hundreds of advertisements and on promotional literature. Nipper himself passed away in 1895 at age eleven, before he had become an international phenomenon. He lives on, however, as one of the most famous trademarks in the world.

Also patterned after real life was Tige, the Boston Terrier who has been helping his master, Buster Brown, sell shoes for the better part of a century. Tige and Buster were cartoon characters created in 1902 by Richard Fenton Outcault, and patterned after his own children and dog. Buster, his sister Mary Jane, and Tige were soon as popular as Charlie Brown and Snoopy became in succeeding generations.

For use as a trademark, the Brown Shoe Company purchased rights to Buster and Tige, and introduced the trademark at the St. Louis World's Fair in 1904. Buster, with his Little Lord Fauntleroy clothes and antic behavior, had already caught the public's fancy, and the trademark was a success. From the time it was introduced until 1915 it was promoted by a succession of midgets dressed like Buster who toured the country with a succession of dogs, all chosen for their likeness to Tige. To this day, Buster Brown shoes are a well-known children's brand, and Tige staunchly continues to endorse them.

Trademark dogs vary as much in personality and style as do any other celebrities. Some pick up pizzazz over time. The Greyhound, for instance, enjoyed dizzying promotion in the sixties, after a rather sedate early life.

The Greyhound trademark came into being when the fledgling bus company was named some sixty years ago. When the Fageol brothers of California completed their first bus, an observer commented, "It's as swift and graceful as a Greyhound," or words to that effect. The manufacturers happily adopted the description, named the company Greyhound, and chose the sleek racing dog as their symbol. Since then, the running Greyhound has appeared on every one of the company's thousands of motor coaches, as well as in its advertising.

Buster and Tige

The name BUSTER BROWN and the pictorial likeness of BUSTER BROWN and the dog Tige are the properties of Brown Group, Inc., the owner of the federally registered BUSTER BROWN trademarks, which has consented to the use of the same herein. Reproduction or other use without its permission is strictly prohibited.

Greyhound Corporation's Official Symbol

The Greyhound Corporation, Greyhound Tower,
Phoenix, Arizona 85077

In 1957, a real dog came into the act; as a sponsor of the Steve Allen Show, Greyhound introduced to the show a live Greyhound, Steverino, which shared the comedian's nickname. Although Steverino was a hit, the name was no longer appropriate when the company discontinued its sponsorship of the show. Subsequently the dog was called Lady Greyhound.

Lady Greyhound made countless personal appearances, almost always wearing her jeweled tiara and necklace, and became immensely popular. She was the only canine ever to be crowned Queen of National Dog Week, a title she retained two years in a row. In 1962, a typical year, Lady Greyhound and her trainer appeared on fifty-one television shows and seventeen radio shows (where she kept her comments brief, of course). She was indispensable at fashion shows in department stores and hotels, and of course at the openings of new bus terminals around the country. She also presided at innumerable baseball, football, and basketball games, and at parades. Like nobility everywhere, she willingly visited schools and orphanages—indeed, anywhere people assembled.

For her achievements, Lady Greyhound was given the degree of Associate in Animal Letters by Moravian College in Bethlehem, Pennsylvania. She won the American Humane Association Award and was chosen as America's canine symbol on World Day for Animals. Each year she lent her help to the March of Dimes and Easter Seal campaigns. With her energy and charm, Lady Greyhound proved to be a peerless star; when she died, Greyhound was unable to find a worthy successor. But, althouth Lady Greyhound is gone, her image remains as the company's symbol.

The corporate mascot for Mack Trucks, like the Greyhound symbol, was not based on a specific dog, but on an imaginative description of the product itself. The Mack AC truck was well-recognized for its toughness and dependability, and in fact the model was produced for twenty-four years after its introduction in 1915. Many Mack trucks served with British and American troops in Europe during World War I, where they earned their nickname; when a lesser vehicle became mired down and immobilized, the British "Tommies" would yell, "Aye, bring in one of those Bulldogs." The name fit; the snub-nosed truck not only performed like a Bulldog, but looked like one.

By 1922, the nickname was being used for all Mack products; the company decided there was promotional value in the Bulldog symbol, and adopted it officially. That year, every Mack truck displayed on its side an engraving of a Bulldog tearing up a manual of hauling costs, framed by the familiar outline of the Mack AC hood.

While these are exceptionally successful canine trademarks, many other dogs have served large companies. They include the black Scottish

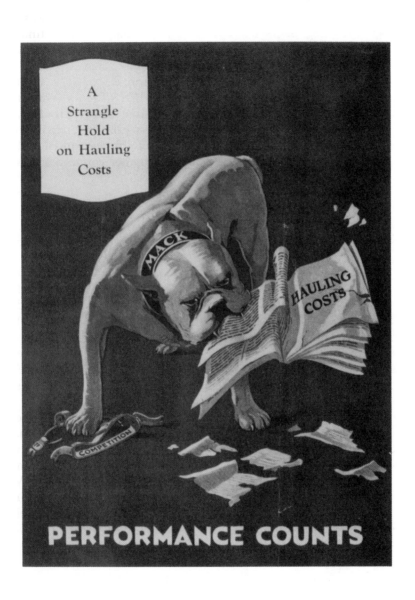

Performance Counts

Terrier and the West Highland White Terrier which symbolize the popular Black and White Scotch whisky. Then there's the doleful Basset Hound who, like Tige, is in the shoe business, endorsing Hush Puppies. Naturally, dogs help sell food. Gaines uses a wide variety of breeds to sell its products, and Recipe dog food uses the Super Star Collie Lassie. Rival uses the world-famous Snoopy, while Kal Kan was promoted by a real celebrity, Frisbee champion Ashley Whippet.

While dog trademarks come and go, RCA's Nipper endures. The first dog to hit Madison Avenue, he is still going strong, perhaps because he stands for one of the traits dog owners prize in their pets: total attentiveness to the master. In any case, among all the canines who serve their companies, Nipper is probably still top dog.

5

Dogs and
Their Native Lands

A good way to creatively name your dog is to go back to the land where the breed was first developed. If, for example, you own a Schnauzer, he hails from Germany, so you might name him Max, Schultz, etc. Get the idea? The following information matches breeds with their native lands. And, if you have a mixed breed, well, you've got a choice of nationalities and names to pick from. . . .

Breed/Native Land

Affenpinscher/*Germany*
Afghan Hound/*Afghanistan and surrounding regions*
Airedale Terrier/*England*
Akita/*Japan*
Alaskan Malamute/*Alaska*
American Foxhound/*United States*
American Staffordshire Terrier/*England*
American Water Spaniel/*United States*
Australian Cattle Dog/*Australia*
Australian Kelpie/*Australia*
Australian Terrier/*Australia*

Breed/Native Land

Basenji/*Central Africa*
Basset Hound/*France*
Beagle/*England*
Bearded Collie/*Scotland*
Bedlington Terrier/*England*
Belgian Malinois/*Belgium*
Belgian Sheepdog/*Belgium*
Belgian Tervuren/*Belgium*
Bernese Mountain Dog/*Switzerland*
Bichon Frise/*Canary Islands*
Black and Tan Coonhound/*United States*
Bloodhound/*Mediterranean area*
Border Terrier/*Scottish-English Border*
Border Collie/*Scottish-English Border*
Borzoi/*Russia*
Boston Terrier/*United States*
Bouvier des Flandres/*Belgium*
Boxer/*Germany*
Briard/*France*
Brittany/*France*
Brussels Griffon/*Belgium*
Bulldog/*England*
Bullmastiff/*England*
Cairn Terrier/*Scotland*
Cardigan Welsh Corgi/*Wales*
Cavalier King Charles Spaniel/*England*
Chesapeake Bay Retriever/*United States*
Chihuahua/*Mexico*
Chinese Shar-Pei/*China*
Chow Chow/*Tibet (developed in China)*
Clumber Spaniel/*England*
Cocker Spaniel/*United States*
Collie (Smooth and Rough)/*Scotland*
Curly-Coated Retriever/*England*
Dachshund/*Germany*
Dalmatian/*Not substantiated*
Dandie Dinmont Terrier/*Scottish-English Border*
Doberman Pinscher/*Germany*
English Cocker Spaniel/*England*
English Foxhound/*England*
English Setter/*England*
English Springer Spaniel/*England*
English Toy Spaniel/*England*

"Mmm, Brittany . . ."

If you're choosing a name for an Australian Terrier, the breed's homeland can be a rich source of many novel and interesting ones.

What could be more German than a Dachshund? If you have a new Dachshund pet or are looking for one, your choice of a name is wide, colorful and more fun than an *Oktoberfest*.

Breed/Native Land

Field Spaniel/*England*
Flat-Coated Retriever/*England*
Fox Terrier (Smooth and Wire)/*England*
French Bulldog/*France*
German Shepherd Dog/*Germany*
German Shorthaired Pointer/*Germany*
German Wirehaired Pointer/*Germany*
Giant Schnauzer/*Germany*
Golden Retriever/*Scotland*
Gordon Setter/*Scotland*
Great Dane/*Germany*
Great Pyrenees/*Pyrenees Mountains*
Greyhound/*Egypt*
Harrier/*England*
Ibizan Hound/*Egypt (transplanted to Ibiza)*
Irish Terrier/*Ireland*
Irish Setter/*Ireland*
Irish Water Spaniel/*Ireland*
Irish Wolfhound/*Ireland*
Italian Greyhound/*Italy*
Japanese Chin/*China (developed in Japan)*
Keeshond/*Holland*
Kerry Blue Terrier/*Ireland*
Komondor/*Mesopotamia (developed in Hungary)*
Kuvasz/*Asia (developed in Hungary)*
Labrador Retriever/*Newfoundland (developed in England)*
Lakeland Terrier/*England*
Lhasa Apso/*Tibet*
Maltese/*Island of Malta*
Manchester Terrier (Standard and Toy)/*England*
Mastiff/*England*
Miniature Bull Terrier/*England*
Miniature Pinscher/*Germany*
Miniature Schnauzer/*Germany*
Newfoundland/*Newfoundland*
Norfolk Terrier/*England*
Norwegian Elkhound/*Norway*
Norwich Terrier/*England*
Old English Sheepdog/*England*
Otter Hound/*England*
Papillon/*Italy*
Pekingese/*China*
Pembroke Welsh Corgi/*Wales*

Breed/Native Land

Pharaoh Hound/*Egypt (transplanted to Malta)*
Pomeranian/*Germany*
Pointer/*Spain (developed in England)*
Poodle (all varieties)/*Russia and Germany*
    (developed in France)
Portuguese Water Dog/*Portugal*
Pug/*China*
Puli/*Hungary*
Rhodesian Ridgeback/*South Africa*
Rottweiler/*Germany*
Saint Bernard/*Switzerland*
Saluki/*Egypt*
Samoyed/*Siberia*
Schipperke/*Belgium*
Scottish Deerhound/*Scotland*
Scottish Terrier/*Scotland*
Sealyham Terrier/*Wales*
Shetland Sheepdog/*Scotland*
Shih Tzu/*China*
Siberian Husky/*Siberia*
Silky Terrier/*Australia*
Skye Terrier/*Scotland*
Soft-Coated Wheaten Terrier/*Ireland*
Spinone Italiano/*Italy*
Staffordshire Bull Terrier/*England*
Standard Schnauzer/*Germany*
Sussex Spaniel/*England*
Tibetan Spaniel/*Tibet*
Tibetan Terrier/*Tibet*
Vizsla/*Hungary*
Weimaraner/*Germany*
Welsh Springer Spaniel/*Wales*
Welsh Terrier/*Wales*
West Highland White Terrier/*Scotland*
Whippet/*England*
Wirehaired Pointing Griffon/*Holland (developed in France)*
Yorkshire Terrier/*England*

The Norwegian Elkhound was the companion of the Vikings and to this day, he retains his rugged handsomeness and love for the outdoors. There are many inspirations for a good name for this fellow.

Drawing by Booth, 1978.

George Booth, the renowned cartoonist whose drawings on cats have become classics, told us, "I don't have a dog—I have five cats. But I *do* have an imaginary dog I call Snarf." Subsequently, he graciously forwarded the above cartoon of Snarf.

6

VIPs and Their Dogs

WHILE there's no law against naming your dog after a Very Important Person (politician, entertainer, business leader, professional athlete, etc.), perhaps it makes more sense to name your dog after the VIP's *dog*! At the very least, we thought you'd like to know the names of some celebrities' dogs.

What's more, we asked them to tell us how they chose the name, with the idea that you might want to know the thought processes they used in naming their pets—so you can apply the same logic (if there *is* any logic involved!).

We are very grateful to the VIPs who shared this information with us. In turn, we understand that many of their dogs appreciate this chance to become celebrities in their own right.

Mary Kay Ash, founder and chairman of the board of Mary Kay Cosmetics, owns a white Toy Poodle named *Gigi*. "My former dog, *Monet,* and Gigi were given to me by a friend. Everyone kept saying that since I was so grieved at the loss of Monet, I shouldn't get another pet quickly. Gigi was the answer. The name Gigi was chosen because it is a French name, and because of the movie *Gigi,* which I had seen years before and loved."

Burt Bacharach and **Carole Bayer Sager**, the Academy Award and Grammy-winning songwriters (and husband and wife) have a female Newfoundland, which they named *Noofy*. The name was selected because everyone always asked what kind of dog their big, black pet is. So, the name helps answer the question.

Erma Bombeck, syndicated newspaper writer, calls her Yorkshire Terrier *Murray*, "because he looked so much like my agent—and I love my agent!"

George Booth, cartoonist, has an "imaginary" dog and tells us how it happened. "*Snarf* is actually my 'imaginary' dog that appears in my drawings in *The New Yorker*. After I created my Bull Terrier several years ago, a gentleman came to my front door with his dog, Snarfi Sue. I liked the name Snarf, and the man gave me permission to use it. It strikes me as a combination of *snarl* and *arf*, and I chose it because *it feels right*. Originally I drew an ornery mutt which was no special breed. People wrote to *The New Yorker* asking whether it was an English Bull Terrier. I began improving his breeding until he is now a full-blooded English Bull Terrier.

Mel Brooks and **Anne Bancroft**, actors, have a Staffordshire Bull Terrier named *Pongo*, because "he just goes pongo."

Patrika Brown, co-owner/founder of The Erotic Baker, has a Lhasa Apso named *Dana*, "after her mother, Miss Disaster" and a Chow/Shepherd mixed breed called *Wolfess*, because "she looks like a wolf—a girl wolf, that is."

Denton Cooley, heart surgeon, owns a Lhasa Apso, *Dalai Lama*, and an English Springer Spaniel, *Atticus*. "My daughter Florence was entranced by Atticus, the main character in the book *To Kill a Mockingbird*. Our Lhasa Apso, with his Tibetan origin, was named Dalai Lama, the name of the spiritual leader of Tibet."

Gary Dahl, inventor of the Pet Rock, calls his German Shepherd *Buckwheat*. "Buckwheat was the only dog of a litter of nine who is all black."

Olivia de Havilland, actress, owns *Shadrach*, an Airedale. "John Huston gave me the dog for a Christmas present. I named him Shadrach for two reasons. First, the name sounds shaggy, and thereby suggestive of an Airedale's coat. Secondly, I chose the name of the biblical character who had undergone great trial and managed to survive."

Phyllis Diller, comedienne, owns a Lhasa Apso called *Phearless*. "The dog was a gift, born to [Mother Dog] Phyllis Diller. The owners chose the pick-of-the-litter, a darling female puppy, who was born in Corsicana, Texas. Mr. and Mrs. O.K. Tate gave me Phearless on New Year's Eve when I was appearing in my third symphony performance [piano] with the Dallas Symphony. I also own a German Shepherd named *Kelly*, a Black Labrador Retriever named *Skipper*, and a Golden Retriever, *Gemima*."

Michael Kirk Douglas, actor, owns *Reggie*, a Jack Russell Terrier. "Reggie's parents were named *Max* and *Ethel*. Their first two pups were named *Mop* and *Flo*. As you can see, I needed a name that was more fitting for my dog. Reggie of Montecito seemed arrogant enough."

Comedienne Phyllis Diller and Phearless

Mary Flatt, founder/owner of Eastern Onion, owns a Doberman Pinscher called *Bone Bone*. "He was so mean-looking that nobody wanted him. Bone seemed to be an appropriate name."

Eileen Fulton, actress, owns a Shih Tzu, *Sarah Bernhardt*, and a Pekingese, *Sir Laurence Olivier*. "They were named after two great stars of the theater."

Freddie Gershon (co-producer of "La Cage Aux Folles," "Grease," "Saturday Night Fever," entertainment lawyer and author) wrote a best-selling book in 1987 titled *Sweetie, Baby, Cookie, Honey*. When his Chinese Shar-Pei was expecting a litter, a sonogram was done to find out how many puppies were present. Since four were due, Gershon and his wife, Myrna, thought they had instant names by using those on the title of his book. But instead of four, there were six pups, so the names *Chickee* and *Darling* were added. The Gershons kept *Cookie* and gave the others to friends, but the original names stayed the same.

Otto Graham, Hall of Fame professional quarterback, owns *Muffin*, a mixed breed (half German Shepherd, half Collie), and *Little Otto*, a Schnauzer. "My daughter named her after another puppy called Muffin who looked like a muff. My son named the Schnauzer after guess who?"

George Hamilton IV, actor, calls his German Shepherd *Loba*, and his Beagle is named *Delilah*. "Loba" means female wolf in Spanish. When our son received this pup as a gift, she was a small pup and mostly black except for a few tan spots. She looked just like a baby wolf—that's how she got her name. When the children brought Delilah home thirteen years ago, we didn't know what to call her. She was a pup, adorable, and we kept trying names. Delilah stuck and fit her perfectly. She wears her name well. She's very proud of it."

Heloise, one of America's most loved syndicated writers, has three dogs, a Schnauzer named *Zinfandel* (called "Zin" for short) because Heloise and David, her husband and pilot, enjoy White Zinfandel wine when they go ballooning in the Heloise Hot Air Balloon. A Keeshond is called *Sheba*, who was named by Heloise's office staff. "Sheba showed up one day at the office and stayed! I was on a book tour so I had no input in naming her." A third dog, a Brittany, is called *Wilhelmina* and nicknamed Willy. She was named after an old hunting dog of David's, and as a puppy she was a Willy-Nilly. To add to the dog's confusion, stepson Russell calls her Willy Wanka!

Bob Hope, entertainer, owns *Snow Job* and *Shadow*, German Shepherds. "Snow Job is a big, beautiful white dog, and Shadow is a black dog. We are an integrated family!"

Jasper Johns, artist, has a mixed breed called *Whiskey*.

Kathy Keeton, president of *OMNI Magazine*, has a Rhodesian Ridgeback, a South African breed, named *Grundy*. Originally from

South Africa, Keeton chose this name because in Zulu it means brave and fearless.

George Kennedy, actor, and his wife Joan, call their Cairn Terrier *Blyme*, and their Maltese is *Buttons*. "We named him Blyme because we brought him back from London. Our other dog, a Maltese, looks like a little button with her tiny nose."

Jean Claude Killy, world champion skier, calls his French Shepherd *Indian*, "because only his ears were visible above a little wall at our house—and they reminded us of Indian feathers."

Elaine and **Jack LaLanne**, physical fitness experts, have a German Shepherd, *Walter*, and a Poodle, *Gnathy*. "Our fourth white German Shepherd was actually named by a television viewer. In a dog-naming contest that awarded the winner a trip to Hawaii, the name Walter was chosen. *We All Love To Exercise Regularly*. We had three other German Shepherds named *Happy*, *Smiley* and *Chuckles*. Another dog is a Poodle named *Gnathy*. A friend who is a gnathostomatist (a dentist who specializes in the mouth and jaw) gave him to us. By the way, you guessed it—Gnathy has a slight overbite."

Suzy Mallery, founder and president of Man Watchers, Inc., calls her Terrier mix *Happy*. "Happy was born in 1975, the year that I founded Man Watchers. Since, in my comedy speeches, I was called the 'Happy Looker,' I named my dog the same. We call her Happy for short—and she is."

Og Mandino, author, owns a Basset Hound, *Slippers*. "Slippers was purchased from a pet shop as a gift to my youngest son, Matthew, for his ninth birthday. Since the puppy had four white paws, Matt immediately named him 'Slippers.' Slippers sleeps in his special chair in my studio when I write, and so my last seven books were written with his nearby assistance."

Stanley Marcus, former CEO of Neiman Marcus Department Store, calls his German Shepherd *Pinon*. "The dog was born in Santa Fe, New Mexico, where the pinon [small pine] tree flourishes. Its wood, when burned, provides the characteristic smell of Santa Fe, and its nuts are delectable when the pinon jays don't get them first."

Cathy Rigby McCoy, gold medal gymnast, calls her Cocker Spaniel *Molly*, because "Molly is Irish enough to go with McCoy."

George McGovern, U.S. Senator and former presidential candidate, has a Newfoundland called *Atticus*. "My daughter, fourteen years old at the time, named him after the character Atticus Finch in Harper Lee's great novel *To Kill a Mockingbird*."

Barry Manilow, entertainer, calls his Beagles *Bagel* and *Biscuit*.

Margrit and **Robert Mondavi**, owners of Robert Mondavi Winery, have a Standard Poodle they call *Fume Blanc*. Mondavi coined the name for a dry Sauvignon Blanc, reversing two French terms, "smoky" and "white." Fume Blanc, the dog, has a smoky, salt-and-pepper coat. By the way, Fume Blanc, the wine, is the winery's top seller, and certainly no dog!

Martina Navratilova, professional tennis player, calls her Fox Terrier *K.D.* "K.D. is short for Killer Dog. On the first day that I brought K.D. home, we were greeted by my other dogs, *Tetsud* and *Ruby*, both medium-sized dogs weighing about twenty-five pounds each. K.D. was only ten weeks old and weighed about two pounds, but when she met the other two dogs, she barked and growled and drove them back. She immediately established her space, and ever since, they leave her alone. Anyway, you can see why I call her K.D."

Jack Nicklaus, professional golfer, and his wife Barbara, have three Golden Retrievers, *Lady, Bear* and *White Paws.* "Lady's official name is 'Lady of Liberty.' We chose this name because her mother was *Liberty*, who was owned by President Ford, and her father's name was *Bart.* Bear is Lady's pup and her official name is 'Lady's Golden Bearoness.' Originally, we tried to think of a clever name that meant 'Bear' in a foreign language, but we ended up with just plain 'Bear.' White Paws is Bear's pup, and, you guessed it, she has white paws!"

Norman Vincent Peale, minister, calls his Golden Retriever *Buff.* "The name 'Buff' describes her coloring. It's short, easy to call—and also lent itself to nicknames."

Greg and **John Rice**, television personalities and professional speakers, own two Irish Setters, *Shane* and *Red.* "When Shane was given to us by a friend, we already had a German Shepherd, *Grit*, named after the John Wayne movie *True Grit.* Grit had a habit of biting Shane's nose, and it actually got to the point where Shane would meekly lie down whenever he'd see Grit. About that time, we saw a movie on television called *Shane*, and the main character was intimidated by some gunmen. The character Shane reminded us of our dog. A funny thing, when we got a second Irish Setter, Shane intimidated him just as he had been intimidated by Grit. We couldn't think of a name (somebody suggested 'Spot,' believe it or not), so we called him Red Dog. Finally we just shortened it to Red, and that's now his official name."

Renee Richards, professional tennis player, owns *Tennis-ee*, an Airedale Terrier, and *Houdini*, a Labrador Retriever. "My Airedale came from a kennel in Tennessee, and he's a tennis dog. So I called him Tennis-ee. My Labrador Retriever is called Houdini because, as a pup, he always escaped from the pen."

Sharon Kay Ritchie, former Miss America, has a Belgian Sheepdog called *Ranu,* because "the dog is black and has a wolf look."

Robert Schuller, minister, calls his Doberman Pinscher *Ambassador,* and his Collie is called *Deacon.* "Ambassador was so named because he prances around our property as if he were somebody very important—like an ambassador. His nickname is 'Amber,' and since he's red, the name is a play on his coloring. Deacon is our Collie, who was named after the football player Deacon Jones. We also have two other dogs—*Pandy*, a German Shepherd named after friends, Paul and Candy, who gave her to us, and *Nicky*, a Samoyed. Nicky is named after St. Nicholas because he is 'white as snow' and was a Christmas present."

David Schwartz, founder/owner of Rent-A-Wreck, calls his mixed breed (half Beagle, half German Shepherd) *Stanley*. "A grammar school principal from New York City rented a Dodge Dart from me, but he wanted to exchange it for a Mustang convertible. I left the car in the lot for him to pick up after closing time, and instructed him where to find the keys. When I arrived at the lot the following morning, a dog was in the back seat. I called Stanley and he replied, 'But I have no dog. I don't know how it got there.' So I called the dog Stanley, and he immediately jumped out of the window and came to me. Stanley has been a happy addition to my family ever since."

Sam Snead, professional golfer, named his Doberman Pinscher *Adam* because "he's a stately looking dog, and I thought the name was fitting and proper."

Alex Stein is the owner of the world-champion Frisbee-catching dog, *Ashley Whippet*. "I call him Ashley Whippet because the breed [Whippet] is from England, so I wanted a distinguished British name."

Strom Thurmond, U.S. Senator, has two Cocker Spaniels, *Lady* and *Tramp*. "The children named the dogs after the Walt Disney characters."

Marilyn Van Derbur, former Miss America, calls her mixed breed *Benji*. "After twenty years of a 'dogless' marriage, our eleven-year-old daughter made it clear that she wanted a dog more than anything else in the whole world. We responded to an ad in the newspapers reading, 'Come get Benji.' We did."

Andy Williams, entertainer, has a Boxer named *Barnaby*, named after the title character in Charles Dickens' novel *Barnaby Rudge*.

Jacklyn Zeman, television actress, owns two German Shepherds, *Ruffian* and *Runner*. "I named my first German Shepherd 'Ruffian' because she loves to lie on her back and wrestle with me. She also loves to play Frisbee, tag, and tug of war. She's rough in that she competes and obviously loves to win, but otherwise she's very gentle. My other German Shepherd was named 'Runner' because that's the very first thing he did when we brought him in—he ran all over the house. He's three years old now—and he still runs all over the house!"

Efrem Zimbalist, Jr., actor, has a German Shorthaired Pointer called *Zimmie*. "With a name like Zimbalist, what else would you name your dog?"

"Here, Eugene . . ."

7

Human Names

T HE following human names, in our opinion, are suitable for your dog. Please note that while you might like a particular name for a person, it just might not be suitable for your pet. Likewise, some human names seem to work out better for dogs than they do for people (*Homer, Dwight, Nellie* and *Gertrude,* for example). Homer is fine for a Basset Hound, but I certainly wouldn't give a kid that handle.

Since there are thousands of human names in the English language, it's important for you to realize that the following male and female lists are limited to 100 each. So please don't be unhappy if your name didn't make it. We simply couldn't include everyone's name. So cheer up, Lois, Nancy, Tom, and Brad—we had to draw the line somewhere!

Female

Abigail
Agatha
Alice
Amy
Anastasia
Annie
Audrey
Bathsheba
Belle
Beulah
Bonnie
Bridget
Brooke
Cassie
Cecilia
Celeste
Clementine
Cleo
Colette
Courtney
Crystal
Dagmar
Dawn
Désirée
Dinah
Dotty
Eloise
Elvira
Emily
Ethel
Evita
Fanny
Fifi
Florence

Flossie
Freda
Gertrude
Ginger
Gracie
Greta
Gwen
Harriet
Hatty
Heidi
Hilda
Jennifer
Jessica
Jill
Josephine
Justine
Kate
Kelly
Kim
Leslie
Libby
Lillian
Lolita
Lorna
Lucy
Mabel
Maggie
Mary Jane
Meg
Millie
Missy
Nanette
Nellie

Nettie
Nicole
Nina
Olga
Patience
Peggy
Penny
Phoebe
Polly
Prudence
Regina
Rhoda
Roxana
Sabrina
Sadie
Shirley
Stephanie
Suzie
Tammy
Tess
Tilly
Tracy
Trixie
Trudy
Ursula
Veronica
Victoria
Vivian
Wendy
Wilma
Winifred
Yvonne
Zelda

Male

Adam
Alex
Alfred
Amos
Andy
Archibald
Archie
Arthur
Barney
Barry
Bart
Benjamin
Billy
Boris
Bruce
Cedric
Charlie
Chuck
Cliff
Conrad
Curtis
Dexter
Dennis
Dudley
Duncan
Dwight
Edward
Eli
Elmer
Emil
Evan
Floyd
Frank
Fred

Fritz
Geoffrey
George
Gomer
Grady
Grant
Harry
Harvey
Henry
Homer
Hubert
Ian
Isaiah
Ivan
Jacques
James
Jason
Jeremy
Jesse
Johnny
Justin
Kenny
Lance
Leon
Leroy
Luke
Malcolm
Marvin
Max
Melvin
Mike
Nathan
Ned

Neil
Nigel
Oliver
Oscar
Otis
Patrick
Perry
Philip
Pierre
Quentin
Ralph
Randy
Roscoe
Rudolph
Rufus
Sam
Seymour
Sidney
Sigmund
Stanley
Teddy
Toby
Tommy
Troy
Victor
Vincent
Virgil
Waldo
Wilbur
Willie
Wyatt
Zachariah
Zachary

8

Human Nicknames

HUMAN nicknames are often good choices for dogs' names; in fact, they may be even more suitable for dogs than for people. In most cases, people are *given* a nickname as an alternative to the name that appears on their birth certificate. But often a nickname is by *choice*—and therefore welcome improvement over one's given name. Here is an assortment of human nicknames, all field-tested on people.

Ace	Bobo	Bugsy
Babe	Boo	Bunky
Babs	Boo-Boo	Bunny
Baby	Boom-Boom	Buster
Babyface	Bozo	Buzz
Bags	Brownie	Champ
Beanie	Bruno	Chickie
Beeper	Bubba	Chico
Biff	Bubbles	Chip
Big Job	Buck	Chubby
Bimbo	Bucko	Chuckie
Bing	Bucky	Cloudy
Blinky	Bud	Cookie
Bo	Buddy	Cotton

Cubby
Cuddles
Curley
Daffy
Daisy
Dimples
Dixie
Dizzy
Dolly
Duffy
Duke
Dusty
Ears
Fats
Flash
Flattop
Flip
Foots
Foxy
Freckles
Freddie
Fritz
Fritzy
Fuzzy
Gabby
Gipper
Gootch
Guy
Hank
Hubba
Ike
Ironsides
Itchy
Jake
Jives
Jock
Jocko
Jo-Jo
Jolly

Junior
Kilroy
Kinks
Kootch
Lard
Mack
Meathead
Moe
Monk
Moose
Muffy
Ollie
Paddy
Painful
Peaches
Pee-Wee
Pig Pen
Pinky
Ponch
Poo
Pookie
Popsie
Porky
Pudge
Pudgy
Puffy
Punk
Punky
Pussyfoot
Queenie
Rex
Ritzy
Rusty
Sadie
Scooter
Sharky
Skip
Slim
Smiley

Smokey
Snowflakes
Snuff
Snuffy
Sonny
Sorrowful
Sparky
Speedy
Spike
Spud
Spunky
Stinky
Stonewall
Stoney
Stud
Taffy
Tank
Tex
Tinker
Tootie
Toots
Tootsie
Trip
Trixie
Tubby
Tuffy
Tutti
Twiggy
Wally
Wheels
Win
Windy
Wink
Woody
Yank
Yankee
Zeke
Zonkers

"Howdy, Tex . . ."

9

State Nicknames

FOR those of you with a lot of state pride, here's a list of state nicknames from which to choose a name for your dog. You might choose one of these names if you have long since moved out-of-state, but want the local folk to be reminded of where your roots are.

State/Nicknames
> Alabama/*Dixie, Lizard, Yellowhammer*
> Alaska/*Eskimo, Frosty*
> Arizona/*Apache, Aztec, Baby, Cooper, Sandy*
> Arkansas/*Bear, Bowie*
> California/*El Dorado, Eureka*
> Colorado/*Rover*
> Connecticut/*Constitution, Nutmeg*
> Delaware/*Diamond, Muskrat*
> Florida/*Gator, Sunshine*
> Georgia/*Crackers, Goober, King, Peach*
> Hawaii/*Aloha, Pineapple*
> Idaho/*Gem, Ida*
> Illinois/*Prairie, Sucker*
> Indiana/*Hoosier*
> Iowa/*Hawkeye*

State/Nicknames

Kansas/*Grasshopper, Jayhawker, Sunflower*
Kentucky/*Bear, Blue, Corncracker*
Louisiana/*Creole, Pelican*
Maine/*Dirigo, Fox, Lumberjack*
Maryland/*Oysters, Thumper*
Massachusetts/*Baked Beans, Bay, Puritan*
Michigan/*Woverine*
Minnesota/*Gopher*
Mississippi/*Bayou, Missy, Tadpole*
Missouri/*Pike, Show Me*
Montana/*Bonanza*
Nebraska/*Bugger, Husker*
New Hampshire/*Granite*
New Jersey/*Clams, Tomato, Mosquito*
New Mexico/*Sunshine*
New York/*Empire, Knickerbocker*
Nevada/*Digger, Miner, Sagehen*
North Carolina/*Tarheel, Tuckoe*
North Dakota/*Flickertail, Sioux*
Ohio/*Buckeye*
Oklahoma/*Boomer, Sooner*
Oregon/*Beaver*
Pennsylvania/*Dutchboy, Keystone, Quaker*
Rhode Island/*Gunflint, Rhoddy*
South Carolina/*Palmetto, Weasel*
South Dakota/*Coyote*
Tennessee/*Butternut, Whelp*
Texas/*Beefy, Cowboy, Longhorn, Ranger, Tex*
Utah/*Saint*
Vermont/*Greeny*
Virginia/*Beadles, Beagles, Cavalier*
Washington/*Chinook*
Washington, D.C./*Cappy, President, Senator*
West Virginia/*Panhandle*
Wisconsin/*Badger*
Wyoming/*Equality, Sage*

10

Food Names

SINCE eating ranks high on practically everyone's list of favorite pastimes, how about naming your dog after something appetizing. Here's some food for thought. . . .

Alfalfa	Buns	Cocoa
Almond	Butterscotch	Coconut
Ambrosia	Cabbage	Coffee
Apples	Candy	Cookie
Applesauce	Cappuccino	Cornflakes
Apricot	Caramel	Cottage Cheese
Avocado	Cashew	Cranberry
Bagel	Chamomile	Cream Cheese
Banana	Cheese Cake	Cucumber
Beefy	Cheesey	Curry
Blintz	Cherry	Custard
Biscuit	Chestnut	Cutlet
Bologna	Chili	Donut
Bouillon	Chocolate	Drumstick
Boysenberry	Chowder	Eclair
Brownie	Cider	Escargot
Brussel Sprouts	Cinnamon	Espresso

Farfel
Flapjack
Fondue
Fruitcake
Fudge
Gingerbread
Gouda
Goulash
Grub
Gumbo
Gumdrop
Hash
Hollandaise
Honey
Honeydew
Jello
Jelly Bean
Juice
Julienne
Ladyfinger
Lasagna
Lettuce
Licorice
Liverwurst
Lo Mein
Loganberry
Lollipop
Lox
Macaroni
Macaroon
Mango
Margarine
Marshmallow
Matzo Ball
Mayonnaise
Meat Ball
Meat Loaf
Melba

Meringue
Mozzarella
Muffin
Mutton
Nacho(s)
Noodles
Nutmeg
Olive
Omelet
Oregano
Pancake
Pasta
Peaches
Peanuts
Pecan
Pepper
Peppercorn
Peppermint
Pepperoni
Pickles
Pineapple
Pistachio
Pizza
Popcorn
Popsicle
Pork Chops
Porterhouse
Potato
Pound Cake
Pretzel
Prune
Pudding
Pumpernickel
Pumpkin
Quiche
Ragout
Raisin
Raspberry

Ravioli
Rhubarb
Roquefort
Rump Roast
Salt
Sarsaparilla
Sassafras
Sauerkraut
Sauté
Scampi
Sherbet
Shortcake
Sloppy Joe
Soufflé
Soy Sauce
Spaghetti
Spice
Strawberry
Stringbean
Strudel
Succotash
Sugar
Sukiyaki
Taco
Taffy
Tamale
Tangerine
Tapioca
Tenderloin
Teriyaki
Tomato
Truffle
Turnip
Waffles
Wiener Schnitzel
Wonton
Yogurt
Zucchini

11

Military Names

FOR military buffs and those of you with old war stories, you may want to consider the following names for your dog:

Ace	Cadet	Derringer
Agent	Chaff	DMZ (Demilitarized
Ajax	Charlie	Zone)
Alpha	Chopper	Duster
Ammo	Clipper	Falcon
Arrow	CO (Commanding	Falconet
AWOL	Officer)	Fighter
Bayonet	Colt	Fireball
Bazooka	Cong	Flintlock
Blip	Conus (Continental	Foxhole
Blooper	United States)	Frag
Bomber	Corporal	Freighter
Booster	Cougar	General
Boot(s)	Cub	Genie
Brickbat	Dagger	GI
Browning	Dart	Glider
Bullet	Dash	Grunt
Bullpup	Delta	Gunflint

"Patton"

Gung Ho
Gunner
Hatch
Hatchet
Hawk
Howitzer
Hustler
Ike
Jeep
Jet
Jupiter
Khaki
Killer
Lance
Launcher
Lifer
Lugar
LZ (Landing Zone)
MacArthur
Mace
Machete
Major
Marlin

Missile
Mortar
MP (Military
    Police)
Musket
Nike
Patton
Pershing
Polaris
Private
Radar
Remington
Rocket
Saber
Sandbag
Sarge
Scout
Sergeant
Sidewinder
Skybolt
Skyhawk
Slick (Type of
    helicopter)

Snafu
Soldier
Springfield
Supersonic
Sword
Tanker
Target
Tartar
Thor
Torpedo
Tracker
Trench
Trooper
Trubo
Voodoo
Waddy
Winchester
Yankee
Zap
Zapper
Zulu

"Pinocchio"

12

Comic Strip Names

A great source of names are those zany characters from the comics. Here is a delightful group of names, some of them still appearing in the funnies and on Saturday morning television; others are long since gone but certainly not forgotten:

Abner	Captain America	Droopy
Andy Gump	Captain Easy	Dumbo
Annie	Captain Marvel	Earthquake McGoon
Archie	Casper	Fearless Fosdick
Bailey	Charlie Brown	Felix
Barnaby	Clarabelle	Ferd'nand
Barney Google	Colonel Blimp	Flash
Batman	Connie	Flossey
Bessy	Daddy Warbucks	Freckles
Blondie	Daffy	Fred Basset
B.O. Plenty	Dagwood	Garth
Bond	Daisy Mae	Gasoline Alley
Bugs	Dennis the Menace	Goofy
Bunky	Doc	Gravel Gertie
Buster	Dr. Strange	Green Hornet
Captain	Doonesbury	Grumpy

Gumby
Hagar
Happy
Happy Hooligan
Hawkeye
Heathcliff
Hercules
Hornet
Huckleberry Hound
Jester
Jiminy Cricket
Jimpy
Joe Palooka
Juggs
Linus
Little Nemo
Lucy
Lulu
Mammy Yokum
Marmaduke
Marvel
Max
Mercury
Merlin
Midnight
Mr. Magoo

Mr. Twiddle
Nancy
Nikki
Nipper
Nippy
Olive Oyl
Peanuts
Penguin
Peppermint Patty
Phantom
Pinocchio
Pip
Pooky
Popeye
Porky
Radar
Raskind
Richie
Riddler
Sad Sack
Sandy
Shadow
Sheena
Sinbad
Skeezix
Skippy

Sleepy
Sluggo
Smitty
Sneezy
Sniffles
Snoopy
Snow White
Spectre
Spirit
Swee' pea
Sylvester
Tarzan
Tinkerbell
Tootsie
Torch
Tracy
Tramp
Tweety
Veronica
Waldo
Wash Tubbs
Wimpy
Yogi Bear
Ziggy
Zoom
Zoor

13

Historical Names

IF today's heroes don't turn you on, how about naming your dog after a grand figure from the past? Many of those names are better known than some of the most famous celebrities of today. And, after all, you have to admit there is something rather classy about a dog who answers to Aristotle, Balzac, Chaucer. . . .

Abel	Beau Brummell	Canterbury
Abbott	Beaumont	Carnegie
Adam	Beethoven	Catherine
Adams	Berkeley	Cervantes
Agatha (Christie)	Bernard (Shaw)	Cézanne
Alexander	Bismarck	Chamberlain
Ansel	Bogart	Chaplin
Anthony	Bonaventure	Chaucer
Archimedes	Brahms	Chopin
Aristotle	Brontë	Churchill
Attila	Bryant	Cicero
Augustine	Byron	Claudius
Bacon	Cabot	Cleopatra
Balboa	Caesar	Cleveland
Balzac	Cain	Clovis

Columbus
Confucius
Constantine
Cortez
Cromwell
Curley
Custer
Dante
Darwin
Degas
Delilah
DeSoto
Dewey
Dickens
Dickinson
Dostoevsky
Edison
El Cid
Elijah
Elizabeth
Elliott
Emerson
Epictetus
Faulkner
Fechner
Franklin
Gable
Gainsborough
Galileo
Gandhi
Gideon
Goethe
Goya
Grant
Groucho
Guido
Hamilton
Hamlet
Harrington
Hardy
Hawthorne
Hemingway
Hippocrates
Homer

Horace
Houdini
Jackson
Jefferson
Jung
Keats
Kennedy
King John
King Tut
Kipling
Lafayette
La Salle
Lautrec
Leonardo
Lincoln
Longfellow
Luther
Macbeth
Madame de
    Pompadour
Madison
Magellan
Mao
Marconi
Marco Polo
Marius
Marquis
Matisse
Maximilian
McCarthy
McKinley
Mellisus
Melville
Mendelssohn
Michelangelo
Milton
Mohammed
Monet
Monroe
Montgomery
Mordecai
Moses
Mozart
Naomi

Napoleon
Nero
Newman
Newton
Nightingale
Noah
Norman
Nostradamus
Obadiah
O'Keefe
Oliver
Orwell
Oscar (Wilde)
Pasteur
Patton
Philo
Picasso
Plato
Plotinus
Plutarch
Poe
Pompey
Pope
Proust
Pyrrhus
Rachel
Raleigh
Ramses
Rebecca
Rembrandt
Remington
Renoir
Reuben
Revere
Richter
Rockefeller
Rodin
Romulus
Rooney
Roosevelt
Rousseau
Rubens
Russell
Ruth

"Napoleon"

Samson	Stonewall	Waldo (Emerson)
Sandburg	Stow	Walt (Whitman)
Sara	T.S. (Eliot)	Washington
Seneca	Tennyson	Watson
Shakespeare	Tiberius	Webster
Sir Isaac (Newton)	Titian	Wendell
Sir Walter	Tolkien	Whistler
(Scott/Raleigh)	Tolstoy	Whitman
Socrates	Valentino	Wilhelm
Solomon	Vanderbilt	Windsor
Spartacus	Van Gogh	Wordsworth
Spinoza	Victoria	Wundt
Steinbeck	Virgil	Zachariah
Stevenson	Voltaire	Zephaniah

14

Mythological Names

IF there's no one in the history books you admire enough to name your dog after, there must be someone or something in mythology that is suitable. Surely your dog deserves to be named after one of the gods. Or if this presumption seems a bit pretentious, perhaps a Roman or Greek hero will fill the bill nicely.

The names listed below have been chosen from Greek, Roman, Norse, Celtic, Slavic and Indian mythology. As you will note, the Greeks and Romans enjoyed a superabundance of gods. In the following list many of the most difficult-to-pronounce names have been excluded —as well as many of the *lesser* gods. Even so, you may have trouble pronouncing some of them.

Name/Description

      Aeolus/*Greek king of the winds.*

      Aesculapius/*Roman god of medicine.*

      Agni/*Indian god of fire.*

      Aphrodite/*Greek goddess of love and beauty.*

      Apollo/*Greek and Roman god of light and music.*

      Ares/*Greek god of war.*

      Argo/*Famous Greek ship which carried Jason in his search for the golden fleece.*

Name/Description

Artemis/*Greek goddess of hunting and childbirth. Also the moon goddess.*

Athena/*Greek goddess of wisdom.*

Aurora/*Roman goddess of the dawn.*

Bacchus/*Roman god of wine.*

Balder/*Norse god of light.*

Castor/*Twin son of the Greek god Zeus. God of boxing, wrestling and equestrian sports.*

Cerberus/*Dog that guarded door of Hades, according to Greek mythology.*

Ceres/*Roman goddess of the harvest.*

Cronos/*Greek ruler of the Titans.*

Cupid/*Roman god of love.*

Cyclops/*Lawless Greek giant with one eye in center of forehead. He forged thunderbolts for Zeus.*

Dagda/*Celtic Irish god of fruitfulness.*

Dazbog/*Slavic sun god.*

Demeter/*Greek goddess of the harvest.*

Diana/*Roman goddess of hunting and childbirth.*

Dionysus/*Greek god of wine.*

Echo/*Greek mountain nymph condemned to almost complete silence. She could only repeat the last words of what anyone said to her. She pined away and nothing was left but her voice, "an echo."*

Eos/*Greek goddess of the dawn.*

Eris/*Greek goddess of discord.*

Eros/*Greek god of love.*

Fortuna/*Greek goddess of fortune.*

Freya/*Norse beloved goddess of spring. (Friday)*

Gaea/*Greek goddess of the earth.*

Hades/*Greek god of the underworld and of the dead.*

Hebe/*Greek goddess of youth and cupbearer of the gods.*

Hecate/*Greek goddess of the dark of the moon and the crossways.*

Hephaestus/*Greek god of fire.*

Hera/*Greek queen of heaven, wife of Zeus.*

Hercules/*Greek hero of great strength and courage.*

Hermes/*Greek messenger of the gods; god of commerce and science and protector of travelers, thieves and vagabonds.*

Hestia/*Greek goddess of the hearth.*

Hypnos/*Greek god of sleep.*

Indra/*Indian storm god; the most powerful god of India.*

Iris/*Greek goddess of the rainbow.*

Name/Description

Janus/*Roman god of beginnings; two-faced, in opposite directions. (January)*

Jason/*Greek hero who built first large ship, Argo, to search for the golden fleece.*

Juno/*Roman queen of the gods, wife of Jupiter. (June)*

Jupiter/*Roman king of the gods.*

Loki/*Mischievous Norse creature who was always playing tricks on the gods.*

Maia/*Roman goddess of spring.*

Mars/*Roman god of war. (March)*

Medusa/*In Greek mythology, a monstrous-headed gorgon so hideous that all who looked at her were turned to stone; slain by Perseus.*

Mercury/*Roman messenger of the gods.*

Minerva/*Roman goddess of wisdom, crafts and war.*

Neptune/*Roman god of the sea.*

Nike/*Greek goddess of victory.*

Odin/*Norse ruler of the universe. One-eyed king of the gods. Also called Woden. (Wednesday)*

Odysseus/*Greek king of Ithaca (Latin Name: Ulysses).*

Oedipus/*In Greek mythology he solved the riddle of the Sphinx, thereby becoming king of Thebes.*

Orpheus/*Greek singer and player of the lyre.*

Pan/*Greek god of fields, forests and wild animals.*

Perun/*Slavic god of thunder.*

Phoenix/*Grecian bird that gave birth to itself and lived for at least 500 years, feeding on perfumes and spices.*

Pluto/*Greek god of the underworld.*

Pollux/*Twin son of the Greek god Zeus. God of boxing, wrestling and equestrian sports.*

Poseidon/*Greek god of the sea.*

Psyche/*Roman princess more beautiful than Venus.*

Saturn/*Roman god of agriculture.*

Siva/*In India, it was believed that Siva would bring an end to the world; god of many attributes.*

Sphinx/*Grecian monster with body of lion, head and breast of a woman.*

Stentor/*Grecian herald used to rally the army because his voice was as loud as fifty men.*

Surya/*Sun god in India.*

Terra/*Roman goddess of the earth.*

Thor/*Biggest and strongest of Norse gods; the thunderer. (Thursday).*

Name/Description

Ulysses/*Latin name for Odysseus, Greek king of island of Ithaca.*

Uranus/*Greek and Roman god of heaven.*

Venus/*Roman goddess of love.*

Vesta/*Roman goddess of the hearth.*

Vulcan/*Roman god of fire.*

Zeus/*Greek king of the gods; ruler of earth and heavens.*

15

British Names

OUR American and Canadian roots go back to England; even today, with the Revolution well behind us, we are still enamored of anything that sounds British. Somebody once said: "Look Irish, think Yiddish, and speak British." So with this in mind, we offer the following "very British" names for your dog's consideration:

Abbott	Cambridge	Dennison
Addison	Canterbury	Dewsbury
Ardley	Carlton	Dover
Ashby	Chamberlain	Dudley
Ashington	Chancellor	Dunston
Avon	Chandler	Edison
Axminster	Chapman	Ellenborough
Baxter	Chatham	Ellery
Bedlington	Chester	Ellison
Bentley	Chippenham	Elsworth
Berkshire	Churchill	Epsom
Birney	Clifford	Essex
Blakeley	Coventry	Farnley
Buckingham	Dempster	Farnsworth
Cadbury	Denly	Fenton

"Churchill"

Fitzgerald
Garfield
Greeley
Grimsby
Hadley
Hamilton
Hardy
Harrison
Hastings
Hunter
Huntington
Huxley
Jefferson
Jennison
Kendall
Kenley
Kenilworth
King
Kingsley
Kingston
Ladworth
Landsbury
Langley
Leighton
Lindell
Madison

Manchester
Marshall
Morrison
Northrop
Norwell
Nottingham
Olney
Orson
Oswald
Oxford
Paddington
Palmer
Prescott
Prince
Queen
Radcliff
Robinson
Rover
Rugby
Rutledge
Seabrook
Sedgwick
Shelby
Spencer
Stafford
Stewart

Stratford
Surrey
Sussex
Sutton
Tennyson
Tewkesbury
Thorpe
Trowbridge
Upton
Wadsworth
Walby
Waller
Waltham
Washington
Wellington
Westcott
Wimbledon
Winchell
Winchester
Windsor
Winston
Winthrop
Worcester
Yarmouth
York
Yorkshire

"Judge"

16

Names Related to Vocation and Avocation

IF you have a special interest in a particular occupation or pastime perhaps you should explore it as a source for your dog's name. After all, your vocation or avocation does consume a large percentage of your time, so it is probably on your mind pretty constantly. If so, and you derive a lot of pleasure from it, why not come up with a name for your dog based on your occupation, or your favorite sport or hobby. Here's a list of things people do at work and play, together with suggestions for possible canine names (pairs are listed in parentheses):

Vocation/Avocation/Names

Accountant/*Ledger, Loophole, Taxi, Write-off (Debit and Credit)*
Actor/*Applause, Curtains, Encore, Limelight, Stage*
Actuarian/*Charts, Stats*
Acupuncturist/*Needles, Pins, Sticks*
Advertising/*Ad, Logo, Spot, Tag*
Allergist/*Gasp, Pollen, Shots, Sneeze, Sniffles, Wheeze*
Art Dealer/Artist/*Art, Brush, Easel, Monet, Painter, Picasso, Primer, Rembrandt, Renoir, Van Gogh*

Vocation/Avocation/Names

Attorney/*Briefs, Custody, Felon, Jeopardy, Judge, Jury, Malice, Mouthpiece, Shyster, Sue, Summons, Verdict*

Auto Repair/*Bumper, Fender, Heavy Duty, Motor, Paint Job, Shine (Nut and Bolt)*

Baker/*Bagel, Cookie, Donut, Doughboy, Eclair, Lady Finger*

Banker/*Bucks, Cash, Cents, Dollar, Money, Prime, Security, Teller, Trust*

Barber/Beautician/*Bangs, Blow Dry, Butch, Buzz, Clip, Clipper, Clips, Flattop, Hair, Haircut, Hairpiece, Pageboy, Pigtail, Ream, Scalper, Shag, Sideburns, Toni, Toupee, Trimmer (Rinse and Wash)*

Bartender/*Barhop, Beefeater, Booze, Boozer, Bouncer, Bourbon, Brandy, Bud, Chivas, Cocktail, Cognac, Coors, Grasshopper, Lush, Manhattan, Martini, Scotch, Vodka, Wallbanger*

Baseball/*Babe, Bats, Bunt, Catcher, Coach, Foul Ball, Home Run, Hooker, Pitcher, Reggie, Shortstop, Slider, Southpaw, Strike*

Basketball/*Dr. J., Dunk, Free Throw, Hook*

Bellman/Doorman/*Bags, Cabs, Page, Rooms, Sky, Skycab, Suitcase, Tips*

Boating/*Anchor, Bells, Captain, Knots, Mate, Port, Putt-Putt, Rudder, Skipper, Starboard*

Book Seller/Librarian/*Books, Bookworm, Browser, Reader*

Bowling/*Alley, Brunswick, Spare, Strike, Tenpin*

Butcher/*Beef, End, Ham, Lean, Meat, Prime, Porterhouse, Ribs, Roast, Sausage, Turkey*

Car Salesman/*Cream Puff, Lemon*

Card Playing/*Ace, Blitz, Bridge, Card, Chips, Clubs, Diamonds, Deuce, Dummy, Gin, Joker, Poker, Rummy, Spades*

Clergyman/*Charity, Faith, Hope, Hymn, Miracle, Pious, Prayer, Saint, Spirit*

Coach/*Champ, Jock*

Clothier/*Bloomers, Bobbysocks, Britches, Button, Clodhopper, Corduroy, Creepers, Cuffs, Denim, Dickey, Gabardine, Jumper, Loafers, Panty-hose, Pockets, Slacks, Trousers, Tweed, Tweedy, Tux, Zipper*

Computer Programmer/*Byte, Bit, Chip, Disk, Keyword, Printout*

Cook/*Calorie, Kettle, Pepper, Spice (Pots and Pans, Sugar and Cream)*

Vocation/Avocation/Names

Dentist/*Caps, Cavity, Drill, Floss, Gargle, Gums, Molar, Mouthwash, Novocaine, Toothache*

Dermatologist/*Pimple, Skin, Zits*

Detective/*Clues, Dick, Holmes, Sherlock*

Direct Sales/*Beauty, Ding-dong, Key, Mary Kay, Master, Soaps, Sponsor*

Disc Jockey/*Disc, Funky, Jazz, Rock*

Dry Cleaner/*Press, Spotty, Steam*

Electrician/*Bulbs, Circuit, Flash, Power, Shorts, Sparks, Sparky, Watts (AC and DC)*

Engineer/*Slide Rule*

Farmer/*Cornpicker, Crop, Haymaker, Hayseed, Plowboy, Reaper, Zeke*

Fireman/Chief, Flame, Smokey

Fishing/*Bait, Carp, Flounder, Sinker, Trout*

Football/*Butkus, Passer, Punt, Spike, Split End, Tackle, Touchdown*

Funeral Director/*Bucket, Stiff*

Gambler/*Blackjack, Bookie, Casino, Craps, Dealer, Dice, Jackpot, Lucky, Poker, Spot, Vegas (Heads and Tails)*

Gardener/*Bud, Crabgrass, Dandelion, Dirt, Greeny, Petunia, Poppy, Rosebud*

Geologist/*Diamond, Dirt, Dirty, Rocky, Silver*

Golfer/*Arnie, Birdie, Bogey, Caddy, Chip, Duffer, Eagle, Flag, Hook, Jack, Links, Par, Putt, Putter, Sammy, Slicer*

Government Bureaucrat/*Politics, Red Tape, Slush Fund*

Grocer/*Cola, Dr. Pepper, Pepsi, Red Pop, Popsicle, Six Pack*

Horses (Riding and Racing)/*Bits, Bronco, Derby, Hoofs, Jockey, Jumper, Mustang, Pacer, Prancer, Prancie, Saddles, Scratch, Silks, Sugar, Trotter, Whip*

Hotel/Motel Operator/*Fleabag, Keys, Lobby*

Housekeeper/*Brooms, Car Pool, Drip Dry, Dusty, Leftovers, Rags, Sheets, Soaps, Towels, Vacuum (Cups and Saucers, Pots and Pans)*

Insurance/*Agent, General, Guardian, Keogh, Lloyds, Met, Premium, Pru, Rider, Risk, Security*

Inventor/*Crackpot, Crank, Patient, Screwball, Wacko, Wacky*

Jeweler/*Carat, Diamond, Emerald, Opal, Pearl, Ruby*

Jogging/*Jogger, Marathon, Nike, Runner*

Junk Dealer/*Crunch, Junkie*

Language Translator/*Comprendo, Repeat*

Locksmith/*Keys, Locks*

Manicurist/*Clipper, Fingers, Nails, Polish, Scissors, Toes*

"Rembrandt"

Vocation/Avocation/Names

Meteorologist/*Comet, Mercury, Star, Venus*

Mountain Climbing/*Peak, Quest, Snowtop, Tops*

Musician/*Brass, Conductor, Jazzy, Notes*

News Reporter/*Beat, Headline, Newsy, Print*

Nurse/*Bedpan, Florence, Nightingale, Scalpels, Shots*

Oil and Gas/*Gasser, Gusher, Rig, Wildcat*

Optometrist/*Contacts, Shades, Specs*

Photographer/*Cheese, Copy, Flash, Lens, Smiles, Snapshot, Zoomer*

Physician/*Aspirin, Casey, Doc, Hippocrates, Kildare, Needles, Pills, Quack, Shots, Welby*

Plastic Surgeon/*Facelift, Nose Job, Scarface, Tummy Tuck*

Plumber/*Drain, Flush, Leaks*

Policeman/*Billy, Bobby, Captain, Copper, Flatfoot, Fuzz, Rookie*

Politician/*Governor, Freedom, Lameduck, Liberty, Lobby, Senator, Stars, Stripes, Victory, Windy, Yankee*

Post Office/*Doorbell, First Class, Parcel, Postmark, Stamps, Walker, ZIP (Rain and Shine)*

Principal/*Boss, Chief*

Prison Guard/Warden/*Bars, Jailbird, Stripes (Ball and Chain)*

Professor/*Egghead, Highbrow, Prof, Teach (Publish and Perish)*

Psychologist/Psychiatrist/*Adler, Ego, Freud, Pavlov, Piaget, Psycho, Shrink, Sigmund, Skitzo*

Public Speaking/*Applause, Circuit, Jokes, Live-wire, Mike, Pep Talk, Speaker, Stand-up*

Publishing/*Author, Chief, Editor, Ghost, Writer*

Racketball/*Handball, Hardball, Hinder, Rackets, Wallbanger*

Railroad Employee/*Caboose, Loco, Porter, Pullman, Rails, Tracks*

Real Estate/*Condo, Deeds, Escrow, High Rise, Lister, Overage, Space, Square Feet*

Retailer/*Clerk, Close Out, Discount, Keystone, Markdown*

Roofer/*Shingles*

Secretary/*Shorthand, Steno, Typo, White-out*

Service Station Employee/*Diesel, Ethyl, Fill-up, Gasser, Greaser, Jumper, Pumper, Pumps (Sparks and Plugs)*

Sex Therapist/*Climax, Couples, Fore Play, Sensation (Birds and Bees)*

Singer/*Harmony, Jazz, Melody, Notes, Rhythm*

Stockbroker/*Barron, Bonds, Capital, Dow Jones, Options, Trader (Bull and Bear, Puts and Calls)*

Vocation/Avocation/Names

Student/*Books, Bookworm, Coed, Cram, Crib Sheet, Dunce, Genius, Grind, Locker, Plebe, Prep, Preppie, Prom, Smarts*

Surgeon/*Cutter, Sawbones, Stitch*

Swimmer/*Backstroke, Butterfly, Chlorine, Dolphin, Fish, Flipper, Fly, Freestyle, Lap, Splash*

Tailor/*Cuff, Thread (Pin and Needle)*

Teacher/*Chalkie, Tardy, Teach (P's and Q's, True and False)*

Telephone Worker/*Bells, Busy, Chime, Hotline, Lineman, Ma Bell, Ring*

Television/*Network, Repeat, Soaps, Sponsor*

Tennis/*Ace, Backhand, Bounce, Doubles, Deuce, Hacker, Lob, Love, Match Point, Net, Point, Racket, Singles, Slam, Top Spin (Serve and Volley)*

Tire Dealer/*Blimp, Chain, Firestone, Flat, Goodyear, Michelin*

Tobacco Dealer/*Nick, Smokey, Weed*

Travel Agent/*Bermuda, First Class, Hawaii, Love Boat, Ticket, Tourist, Trip*

Truck Driver/*C.B., Cabbie, Four-Wheeler, Mack, Overdrive, Sleepy, Teamster, Truck, Wheels*

Waiter/Waitress/*Napkin, Short-order, Tip*

Weight Lifting/*Biceps, Brute, Hulk, Iron, Jerk, Muscles, Press, Pump*

Writer/*Alias, Best Seller, Bookmark, Deadline, Footnote, Ghost, Hack, Hacker, Hemingway, Shakespeare, Thesaurus*

17

Yiddish Names

IF you want your dog to have an international name, *think Yiddish*. In fact, it's not a bad idea to teach your dog to think Yiddish. He may be easier to train. The following is a wide selection of popular Yiddish words (heard frequently on "The Tonight Show" and other talk shows). And for those of you who don't speak the language, brief definitions are included:

Name/Meaning
>   Badchen/*a jester*
>   Bagel/*a round bread similar to a doughnut, but hard*
>   Balebos/*the big boss*
>   Baren/*bother*
>   Batlen/*egghead*
>   Boytshik/*little boy; affectionate term for boy or man*
>   Borsht/*beet or cabbage soup*
>   Bubu/*mistake*
>   Chai/*life*
>   Challeh/*a braided bread*
>   Chazer/*a pig*
>   Chutzpeh/*brazenness; gall*
>   Draykop/*scatterbrain*

Name/Meaning

Eyzel/*Fool* (literally, a donkey)
Feygele/*little bird*
Farfel/*noodles*
Farmisht/*mixed up; confused*
Ferd/*a fool (literally, a horse)*
Focha/*a fan*
Foygel/*a smart guy*
Foyler/*lazy man*
Fremder/*a stranger*
Freser/*a big eater*
Ganev/*crook*
Gazlen/*robber*
Gelibteh/*beloved*
Gelt/*money*
Glik/*good luck*
Goylem/*a dull person*
Heloish/*brave*
Hitsik/*hothead*
Kalyekeh/*misfit*
Karger/*miser*
Kemfer/*fighter*
Klutz/*clumsy person*
Knacker/*show-off*
Kugel/*pudding*
Landsman/*countryman*
Lox/*smoked salmon*
Makher/*big shot*
Meydel/*unmarried girl*
Meyvin/*an expert*
Mazel Tov/*good luck; congratulations*
Mekler/*stockbroker*
Mentsh/*an honorable, decent man*
Meshugass/*crazy antics*
Meshuge/*crazy*
Mieskeit/*ugly thing or person*
Mogen Dovid/*David's shield*
Mumcheh/*expert*
Naches/*joy*
Nebish/*awkward person*
Nishtiskeit/*a nobody*
Nudge/*badger; annoy*
Pupik/*navel; bellybutton*
Pushke/*poor box*

"Shmulky—Sad Sack"

Names/Meaning

Rayk/*rich*

Rosheh/*a mean, evil person*

Seykhel/*good sense*

Shnaps/*whiskey*

Shnorer/*a moocher*

Shtiklech/*tricks*

Shadkhen/*a matchmaker*

Sheynkayt/*beauty*

Shalom/*peace*

Shammes/*a sexton or beadle in a synagogue*

Shiker/*a drunk person*

Shlep/*drag*

Shlepper/*sloppy, clumsy person*

Shlemazel/*unlucky person*

Shlump/*untidy person*

Shmalts/*grease or fat*

Shmaltsy/*nostalgic; sentimental*

Shmulky/*a sad sack*

Shoyman/*a watchman*

Tokhes/*fanny*

Tumler/*a noisemaker*

Zaftik/*well-stacked (woman)*

Zeyde/*grandfather*

Zelig/*blessed*

Zhlob/*a jerk*

Ziskeit/*sweet thing (endearing term for child)*

18

European Names

Y OU might want to name your dog with a European name after his or her country of origin, or perhaps yours. What's more, they sound so continental. . . .

Aaftink	Christa	Ermano
Adrian	Christoph	Ervina
Alain	Claudio	Eva
Alberto	Corinne	Felice
Alexei	Denis	Florian
Anatoli	Domenico	Franck
Andrea	Domingo	Francois
Angelotti	Donati	Friedrick
Anton	Dorota	Frode
Antonio	Dusan	Gabi
Arrigo	Eamon	Gabriel
Bakari	Eduardo	Garcia
Bogdan	Eirik	Georges
Bruno	Elvira	Giacomo
Carlo	Emmanuel	Gisele
Cerstin	Engelbert	Giulio
Cesar	Erik	Giuseppe

Gorrio
Gottlief
Grega
Gretel
Guenter
Guido
Gunde
Gunther
Gustave
Hanni
Hans
Heinrich
Heikki
Henri
Hermit
Herod
Herve
Holger
Hugo
Hussain
Ida
Igor
Ingemar
Ingo
Irike
Jacopo
Jan
Jani
Janos
Javier
Jiri
Jochen
Joerg
Johann
Jules

Karin
Katarina
Kinshofer
Klaus
Kurt
Lars
Leif
Leopold
Lola
Lorenzo
Lucia
Luciano
Ludwig
Manfred
Manuel
Marcel
Marcello
Marco
Marguerite
Maris
Martina
Mateji
Matti
Mattias
Maurilio
Mercedes
Michel
Michela
Mikala
Mikhail
Mojca
Mustafa
Nanetta
Nicoletta

Nicolo
Olafs
Ole
Otello
Pacal
Paoletta
Pasquale
Philippe
Pierre
Pietro
Radim
Reginald
Reinhart
Roderich
Rosi
Ruggero
Salvatore
Serge
Sergei
Sergio
Sigrid
Stefan
Stefano
Stephan
Tamara
Tomas
Torgeir
Torgney
Uwe
Vegard
Vida
Vladimar
Werner
Yvonne

19

Long-Hair Dogs

HAVE a dog with long hair? Why not a name of a famous long-hair artist, composer, philosopher, etc.

Anaximenes	Cicero	Fiorello
Aristotle	Confucius	Franklin
Bach	Dali	Freud
Bacon	da Vinci	Gainsborough
Beethoven	Darwin	Galbraith
Berkeley	Degas	Galileo
Bellows	Descartes	Gilson
Bizet	Dewey	Giotto
Bonaventura	Donizetti	Gounod
Botticelli	Duchamp	Goya
Brahms	Edison	Grotius
Braque	Einstein	Handel
Cellini	El Greco	Hegel
Cezanne	Engels	Heraclitus
Chagall	Epictetus	Hobbes
Chardin	Epicurus	Hume
Chaucer	Falstaff	Jaspers
Chopin	Figaro	Jefferson

Kandinsky	Poussin	Soutine
Klee	Puccini	Spencer
Longfellow	Raphael	Spinoza
Lucretius	Redon	Strauss
Manet	Rembrandt	Thales
Masson	Renoir	Theophrastus
Matisse	Rockwell	Toulouse-Lautrec
Mendelssohn	Rodan	Tschaikowsky
Michelangelo	Romney	Turner
Monet	Rousseau	Utrillo
Mozart	Rubens	Vandyke
Nietzsche	Rossini	van Eyck
Otello	Sandburg	van Gogh
Pavarotti	Schubert	Velasquez
Philo	Schopenhauer	Verdi
Picabia	Seneca	Vuillard
Picasso	Shelley	Wagner
Pizarro	Signac	Whistler
Plato	Sisley	Whitman
Poe	Socrates	Wordsworth

20

Names for Specific Breeds

CHOOSING a name according to the breed of your dog is a way to pick a name. The following is a partial list of a few names for thirty different breeds plus some names for a mixed breed:

Afghan Hound/*Highness, Majesty, Prince, Rapunzel*
Airedale Terrier/*Brillo, Curly, Rex*
Basset Hound/*Sad Sack, Sorrowful, Speedy, Turtle*
Bloodhound/*Dick Tracy, Sherlock, Tracks*
Boston Terrier/*Beans, Pops, Revere*
Borzoi/*Bori, Boris, Ivan, Olga, Romanoff, Yuri*
Boxer/*Ali, Cauliflower, Dempsey, Fighter, Lightweight, Rocky, Slugger, Sugar Ray*
Bulldog/*Bully, Butkus, Chew-Chew, J. Edgar Hoover, Jaws, Jowls, Mack, Meanie, Toughie*
Bullmastiff/*Hulk, Jumbo, Stonehenge*
Chihuahua/*Chi-Chi, José, Loco, Senor, Senorita, Xavier*
Cocker Spaniel/*Flash, Gunner, Slipper, Woody*
Coonhound/*Bootleg, Moonshine*
Dachshund/*Legs, Shorty, Stretch, Stubby, Stump*
Dalmatian/*Domino, Fireball, Pepper*
German Shepherd/*Copper, Flatfoot, Fritz, Fuzz, Max*

"Punchy"

Golden Retriever/*Goldfinger, Midas*

Great Dane/*Awesome, Beaut, Colossal, Gargantua, Hoss*

Greyhound/*Racer, Racy, Speedy, Toothpick*

Irish Setter/*Carrot Top, Old Red, Red, Redtop, Rusty*

Kerry Blue Terrier/*Tru, True Blue*

Labrador Retriever/*Midnight, Sunspot, Splash, Diver, Chip, Cocoa, Hershey, Nestle*

Lhasa Apso/*Lutely* (I abso*lutely* must have that dog!), *Pillow*

Mixed Breed/*Blooper, Blunder, Bonehead, Boner, Boo-boo, Faux pas, Goof, Mistake, Oops, Troubles*

Old English Sheepdog/*Bear, Hippy, Paddington*

Pekingese/*Ching, Chop Suey, Chow, Eggroll, Mao*

Pointer/*Stoolie*

Poodle/*Gigi, Jacques, Dancer, Show-off*

Schnauzer/*Gesundheit*

Scottish Terrier/*Bonnie, Kilts, Kilty, Meg, Meggie*

West Highland White Terrier/*Chivas, Dewar's*

Wire Fox Terrier/*Needles, Bristles*

"Bonnie and Clyde"

21

Names for
Pairs of Dogs

TODAY, in addition to two-car and two-television households, there are also two-dog families. If you are so fortunate as to own a pair, here are some suggestions for naming them:

Abbott and Costello
AC and DC
Adam and Eve
Agony and Ecstasy
Amos and Andy
Antony and Cleopatra
Bagel and Lox
Ball and Chain
Batman and Robin
Beauty and Beast
Blondie and Dagwood
Bonnie and Clyde
Bow and Arrow
Bull and Bear
Buttons and Bows

By and Large
Cheech and Chong
Cowboy and Cowgirl
Cowboy and Indian
Currier and Ives
Cut and Dry
Donny and Marie
Dot and Carrie
Dot and Dash
Duke and Duchess
Franks and Beans
Garbo and Gable
Gilbert and Sullivan
Gin and Juice
Gin and Tonic

Gin and Vodka
Good and Plenty
Ham and Eggs
Hans and Fritz
Hansel and Gretel
Head and Shoulders
Heads and Tails
Heckle and Jeckle
High and Dry
His and Hers
Hit and Miss
Hocus and Pocus
Hugs and Kisses
Hunt and Peck
Jack and Jill
Jekyl and Hyde
Ken and Barbie
King and Queen
Lady and Tramp
Laurel and Hardy
Martini and Rossi
Mickey and Minnie
Milk and Honey
Moon and Sun
Mork and Mindy
Mover and Shaker
Mutt and Jeff
Nice and Easy
Night and Day
Nip and Tuck
North and South
Over and Out
Ozzie and Harriet

Part and Parcel
Pins and Needles
Plus and Minus
Porgy and Bess
Prince and Pauper
Prince and Princess
Punch and Judy
Puts and Calls
Rain and Shine
Razz and Tazz
Remus and Romulus
Rock and Roll
Rodgers and Hammerstein
Rosencrantz and Guildenstern
Rum and Coke
Salt and Pepper
Scotch and Soda
Shirley and LaVerne
Shoes and Socks
Show and Tell
Silver and Gold
Simon and Garfunkel
Skin and Bones
Song and Dance
Stars and Stripes
Sticks and Stones
Sugar and Spice
Tarzan and Jane
Tooth and Nail
Tweedledee and Tweedledum
Vodka and Tonic
Willie and Joe
Yin and Yang

For those of you who belong to three-dog familier, here are a few suggestions for triplets (identical or fraternal):

Bell, Book and Candle
Hook, Line and Sinker
Huey, Dewey and Louie
Larry, Curley and Moe
Shake, Rattle and Roll
Snap, Crackle and Pop

22

Special
Occasions Names

IF your dog arrived on a special occasion, such as a birthday, going away or Christmas, you could name it accordingly. The following special occasions offer a variety of choices:

Anniversary/*Beau, Cherub, Crush, Diamond, Gold, Goo-Goo, Happy, Jewel, Lambkin, Love, Lover, Precious, Silver, Snookums, Spooney, Sweetheart*

Bar Matzvah/*Joy, Little Man, Mitzvah, Pub, Thirteen, Whippersnapper*

Birthday/*Baby, Happy, Old Lady, Old Man, Surprise*

Christmas/*Comet, Dancer, Frosty, Holly, HoHo, Jingle, Jolly, Klaus, Kris Kringle, Mistletoe, Prancer, Rudolph, Santa, Scrooge, Snow, Vixen*

Father's Day/*Daddy, Daddy-O, Old Man, Papa, Pops*

Fourth of July/*Banner, Blue, Cracker, Eagle, Flag, Patriot, Sam, Star, Stripes*

Going Away/*Adieu, Adios, Aloha, Au Revoir, Bon Voyage, Bye-Bye, Cheerio, Sayonara, Skiddoo, Skedaddle, Vamoose, Wiedersehen*

"Bon Voyage"

Graduation/*Brains, Cappy, Scholar, Smarts, Yippie*
Hanukkah/*Liberty, Miracle*
Halloween/*Candy, Ghost, Goblin, Jack, Pumpkin, Treat, Trick*
Mother's Day/*Mama, Mom, Old Lady*
Promotion/*Baron, Big Shot, Big Wheel, Bigwig, Chief, Heavy, King, Mogul, Mugwump, Promo, Star, Tycoon, VIP*
Retirement/*Autumn, Crony, Dusty, Fogy, Fossil, Fuddy-Duddy, Granny, Gray, Methuselah, Old Man, Passée, Stodgy, Stuffy*
Thanksgiving/*Cranberry, November, Pilgrim, Pocahontas, Pumpkin, Turkey*
Valentine's Day/*Amour, Capone, Casanova, Cupid, Darling, Don Juan, Eros, Flame, Hearts, Love, Lovebird, Lover, Romeo, Saint, Spooner, Turtledove, Valentine, Venus*
Wedding/*Bliss, Forever, Honor, Joy, Love, Steady*
Welcome Home/*Banzai, Bienvenue, Bon Soir, Cheerio, Greetings, Hello, Howdy, Shalom*

Note: Don't forget: every day is a special occasion. So, you might select a day of the week (except Wednesday and Saturday), or you might choose a month (but not February, October or December). Or you may choose to name your dog according to its sign—Aquarius, Aries, Capricorn, Gemini, Leo, Libra, Pisces, Sagittarius, Scorpio, Taurus or Virgo. (Cancer, however, is not considered an appropriate name for your dog, but you could use *Crab* or *Crabbie* after the sign of the zodiac.)

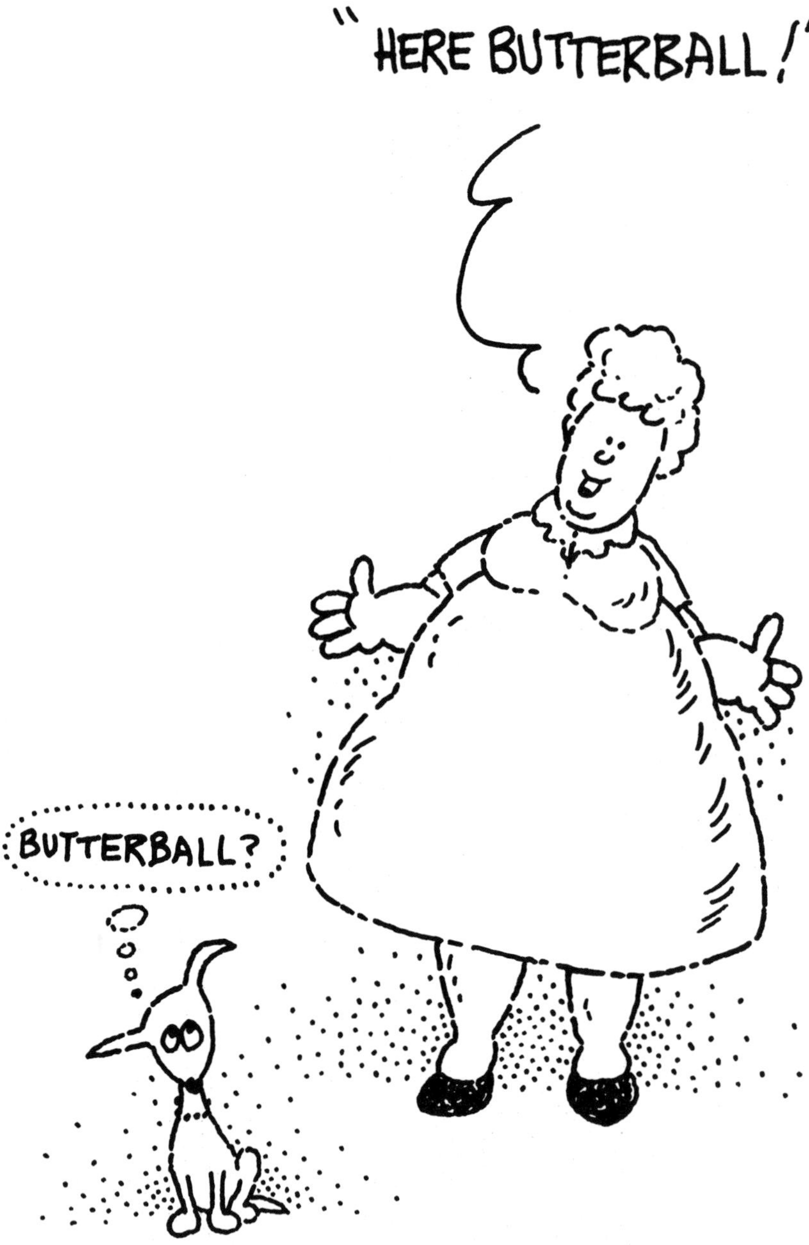
"HERE BUTTERBALL!"
BUTTERBALL?

23

Names for Kids
or Kids at Heart

MANY dog owners relish the naming process of a new dog. Children and adults both contemplate their favorite choice for the dog that will be their friend for years to come. The following examples are characters from literature, cartoons, TV series and other sources with which today's children or yesterday's children will readily identify.

Anastasia and **Drizella**   Cinderella's two evil step sisters.

Barbie   The Mattell Inc. teenage doll whose friends are Kelly, Skipper, Francie, P.J. and Ken.

Barnabus Collins   The 200-year-old vampire on the TV series "Dark Shadows."

Barney Rubble   Fred Flintstone's next-door-neighbor in the popular cartoon series, "The Flintstones." Barney's voice was supplied by Mel Blanc.

Berta   The Siberian cheesehound in the comic strip "Boob McNutt."

Bijou, Sam and **Muffin**   The pet dogs on the TV series "Apple's Way."

Bruno   Cinderella's dog.

Cadbury   The butler in the cartoon series "Richie Rich."

Caesar   Derek Flint's watchdog in the movie "Our Man Flint."

Casper   The friendly ghost who was a TV/comic strip character. Casper debuted in 1946 in a cartoon titled, "The Friendly Ghost." The Apollo 16 command module was named Casper.

Chip 'n' Dale   The mischievous cartoon chipmunks.

Clarabell   The horn-blowing, red-haired clown in the TV series "Howdy Doody," played by Bob Keeshan, who later played Captain Kangaroo.

Cleopatra   The Addams' family's man-eating plant on the television series "The Addams Family."

Cookie Monster   The creature who craves cookies on Sesame Street. His birthday is November 2nd.

Corky, Ching Ching and Rowdy   The three dogs that Shirley Temple owned as a child. Breeds were, in order: Scottie, Pekingese and a Cocker Spaniel.

"The Cosby Kids"   The cartoon series starring characters all with Bill Cosby's voice were named: **Fat Albert, Russell, Dumb Donald, Rudy, Mushmouth, Weird Harold** and **Bucky.**

Daisy   The dog owned by Dagwood and Blondie Bumstead in the cartoon strip "Blondie."

Daisy Moses   The real name of "Granny" on the television series "Beverly Hillbillies."

Dinny   Alley Oop's pet dinosaur.

Ditto   The son in the cartoon "Hi and Lois."

Dobie Gillis   The lead character in the TV series "The Many Loves of Dobie Gillis."

Dot   Ditto's twin sister in the cartoon "Hi and Lois."

Dr. Seuss   The pen name of Theodore Giesel, author of the Dr. Seuss children's books.

Duke   The hound owned by the Clampetts in the TV series "The Beverly Hillbillies."

Dusty   The dog in the cartoon series "Henry."

Glinda   The good witch of the north in the movie "The Wizard of Oz," played by Billie Burke.

Gumby   The plastic toy man whose horse is named Pokey.

Heidi Doody   Howdy Doody's sister on the TV series "Howdy Doody."

Herb and **Tootsie**   Dagwood and Blondie Bumstead's neighbors in the comic strip "Blondie."

Herbert   Pet plant in the TV series "Switch."

Herbie   The Volkswagen in the Disney movie, "The Love Bug."

Herman   The first name of Fred Gwynne's character in "The Munster Family" television series.

Higgins The dog in the TV series "Pettycoat Junction." The same dog also played the title role in the movie "Benji" in 1975.

Homer Pet black widow spider on "The Addams Family" TV series.

Horton The egg-hatching elephant in the story by Dr. Seuss.

Icky and **Dinky** Nephews of the famous cartoon character, Felix the Cat.

Jacko The reversible dog, and one of Jack Bunyan's three dogs.

Little John Robin Hood's sidekick and one of his band of Merry Men.

Long Tom Captain Hook's ship's cannon in *Peter Pan* by James M. Barrie.

Manners The six-inch-high Kleenex Napkin butler used in TV commercials.

Munchkins The little people who lived in Munchkinland in the film, "The Wizard of Oz."

Mr. Peanut The Planters Peanuts trademark.

Mr. Peabody The dog with the genius IQ who partners with a boy named Sherman on the cartoon series "Mr. Peabody," with the trademark, "every dog should have a boy."

Mr. Sanders The name over the door at Winnie the Pooh's house.

Oscar the Grouch The Sesame Street character who lives in a trash can and is always grouchy. The puppet's birthday is June 1st, and its voice is that of Carroll Spinney.

Pete The dog with the ring around his left eye in the "Our Gang" comedy series.

Ruff Dennis the Menace's pet dog's name, who, incidentally, is afraid of cats.

Sam Hondo Lane's (John Wayne) pet dog in the 1954 movie, "Hondo."

Sammy's Shadow The real dog who played the canine lead in the Disney movie, "The Shaggy Dog."

Scraps The dog that co-stars with Charlie Chaplin in the 1918 movie "A Dog's Life."

Scruffy The family dog of the Muirs in the TV series "The Ghost and Mrs. Muir."

Sheena The name of the comic strip character in "Sheena, Queen of the Jungle."

Smiley The shaggy dog of the Baxter family in the TV series "Hazel."

Snuffleupagus The large blue elephant-like character in Sesame Street that only Big Bird can see. His birthday is on August 19th.

Speedy The Alka-Seltzer character created by Robert Watkins in 1952 for the product's TV commercial.

Spike   Creator of Peanuts comic strip, Charles Schultz's real dog who appeared in "Ripley's Believe It or Not" for eating many unusual things.

Spitz   Buck's canine rival in Jack London's *The Call of the Wild*. In the 1935 movie with Clark Gable, Buck's rival is named Prince.

Strip   Tiger's dog in the comic strip "Tiger."

Sylvester   Professor Marvel's horse in the 1939 movie, "The Wizard of Oz."

Tabitha   Samantha and Darrin Stephen's little witch daughter in the TV series "Bewitched."

Tackhammer   Woody Woodpecker's canine foe in the comics.

Tango   Captain Christopher Pike's horse in his youth ("Star Trek" TV series).

Teresa (Tracy) Draco   James Bond's wife for a brief time in Ian Fleming's novel *On Her Majesty's Secret Service*.

Terry Lee   Hero of Milt Caniff's comic strip "Terry and the Pirates."

Toby   Dog in the "Punch and Judy" puppet show.

Tonto   The Lone Ranger's faithful Indian companion. On TV played by Jay Silverheels, a genuine Mohawk Indian.

Useless   Sundance's (Earl Holliman) pet dog in the TV series "Hotel de Paree."

Valda   Secretary to private eye Mike Hammer.

Vulcan   Jean Laffite's pirate ship in the movie "The Buccaneer."

Waldo   Mr. Magoo's nephew in movie cartoons.

Wally   Beaver's older brother in the TV series "Leave It To Beaver."

Wasp   Comic strip nemesis of Mandrake the Magician.

Weary Willie   Sad-faced clown portrayed by Emmett Kelly. Kelly portrayed himself in the 1952 movie "The Greatest Show on Earth."

Wessex   Thomas Hardy's dog.

Whitey   Boston Blackie's little black terrier in "Boston Blackie" on TV.

Wilbur   Fern's little pig, saved by Charlotte the spider in E. B. White's *Charlotte's Web*.

Zorro   Don Diego de Vega, a California Robin Hood, created by Johnston McCulley in the story "The Curse of Capistrano" (retitled "The Mark of Zorro").

24

Memorable Characters from Literature

FOR those of you who are book lovers, here are some memorable fictional characters to name your dog after. Please note that, with a few exceptions, we have limited this chapter to American and English literature. Even so, with so many great books to choose from, it's impossible to include everybody's favorite character. *What to Name Your Dog* wouldn't be complete, however, if we didn't at least tease you with a few illustrious names, so that you might consider literature as a source for your pet's name.

The Age of Innocence
Edith Wharton (1920)
    Archer
    Beaufort
    Dallas
    Newland
    Welland

Alice in Wonderland
Lewis Carroll (1865)
    Alice
    Cheshire
    Dinah
    Duchess
    Elsie
    Lacie
    Mad Hatter
    Tillie

All the King's Men
Robert Penn Warren (1946)
Duffy
Jack
Sadie
Willie

All's Well That Ends Well
William Shakespeare (1602)
Bertram
Duke
Helena

The American
Henry James (1877)
Newman
Tristram

Anna Karenina
Count Leo Tolstoy (1875)
Agatha
Alexander
Constantine
Countess
Karenina
Nicholas
Petrov
Prince

Antony and Cleopatra
William Shakespeare (1607)
Alexas
Antony
Caesar
Charmian
Cleopatra
Demetrius
Iras
Marcus
Octavius

As I Lay Dying
William Faulkner (1930)
Addie
Bundren
Cash
Darl
Dewey
Jewel
Peabody
Vernon
Whitfield

As You Like It
William Shakespeare (1599)
Audrey
Celia
Dennis
Jaques
Le Beau
Oliver
Orlando
Rosalind

The Barber of Seville
Pierre A.C. de Beaumarchais (1775)
Almaviva
Bazile
Figaro
Rosine

Barnaby Rudge
Charles Dickens (1841)
Barnaby
Chester
Daisy
Dolly
Emma
Gabriel
Gashford
Geoffrey
Gordon
Haredale
Langdale
Simon

"Rudolph"

The Beggar's Opera
John Gay (1728)
- Captain
- Jemmy
- Lucy
- Macheath
- Molly
- Polly Peachum

Ben Hur: A Tale of the Christ
Lew Wallace (1880)
- Ben Hur
- Esther
- Messala
- Quintus Arrius
- Simonides

Beowulf
Unknown (1000 A.D.)
- Beowulf
- Grendel
- Hrothgar
- Unferth
- Wiglaf

Between the Acts
Virginia Woolf (1941)
- Bartholomew
- Eliza
- Oliver
- Otter
- Rupert

Bleak House
Charles Dickens (1852)
- Badger
- Barbary
- Bartholmew
- Guppy
- Jarndyce
- Jo
- Snagsby
- Summerson
- Toughey
- Wisk

Brideshead Revisited
Evelyn Waugh (1945)
- Bridey
- Cara
- Cordelia
- Johnjohn
- MacKay
- Marchmain
- Marguis
- Rex
- Ryder
- Sebastian

Call of the Wild
Jack London (1903)
- Buck
- Spitz
- Thornton

Candida
Bernard Shaw (1897)
- Burgess
- Candida
- Eugene
- Fluffy
- Lexy

Candide
Voltaire (1759)
- Baron
- Candide
- Jacques
- Pangloss
- Paquette
- Thunder

The Canterbury Tales
Geoffrey Chaucer (1391)
- Bailey
- Canon
- Chaucer
- Friar
- Knight
- Miller

Monk
Oswald
Parson
Prioress
Sergeant
Squire
Yeoman

Captains Courageous
Rudyard Kipling (1897)
Disko
Harvey
Long Jack
Salters
Troop

Carmen
Prosper Mérimée (1845)
Carmen
Don Jose
Garcia
Lucas
Pancaire

A Christmas Carol
Charles Dickens (1843)
Ebenezer
Marley
Scrooge
Tiny Tim

The Comedy of Errors
William Shakespeare (1592)
Angelo
Pinch

The Count of Monte Cristo
Alexandre Dumas (1844)
Baron
Benedetto
Beauchamp
Count
Countess
Dantes

Fernard
Giovanni
Lord Wilmore
Luigi
Marquis Bartolomeo
Maximilian
Mercedes
Peppino
Valentine

The Damnation of Theron Ware
Harold Frederic (1896)
Alice
Celia
Soulsby

David Copperfield
Charles Dickens (1849)
Babley
Barkis
Clara
Copperfield
Ham Peggotty
Jorkens
Littimer
Little Emily
Lucy
Mealy Potatoes
Mowcher
Sophy
Traddles
Uriah
Wilkins

Death of a Salesman
Arthur Miller (1949)
Ben
Bernard
Biff
Charley
Happy
Willy

The Deerslayer
James Fenimore Cooper
  (1841)
  Captain
  Chingachgook
  Deerslayer
  Hetty Hutter
  Hurry Harry
  Natty Bumppo
  Wah-ta!-Wah

Don Juan
Lord Byron (1819)
  Baba
  José
  Juan
  Donna Inez
  Dudu
  General Suwarrow
  Lambro
  Lolah
  Zoe

Don Quixote
Miguel de Cervantes Saavedra
  (1605)
  Don Quixote
  Sancho Panza

Finnegan's Wake
James Joyce (1939)
  Finnegan
  Humphrey
  Isobel
  Plurabelle

For Whom the Bell Tolls
Ernest Hemingway (1940)
  Fernando
  Jordan
  Maria
  Pablo
  Pilar

Gone with the Wind
Margaret Mitchell (1936)
  Ashley
  Bonnie Blue
  Mammy
  Melanie
  Rhett
  Scarlett

Goodbye, Mr. Chips
James Hilton (1933)
  Chips
  Colleq
  Linford
  Ralston
  Wetherby

The Grapes of Wrath
John Steinbeck (1939)
  Casy
  Jessie
  Joad
  Noah
  Rawley
  Ruthie
  Sairy
  Wilkie

Great Expectations
Charles Dickens (1860)
  Abel
  Bertley
  Biddy
  Gargery
  Havisham
  Jaggers
  Pepper
  Pip
  Startop

The Great Gatsby
F. Scott Fitzgerald (1925)
  Daisy
  Gatsby

"Lancelot"

Jordan
Myrtle
Nick
Wolfsheim

Gulliver's Travels
Jonathan Swift (1726)
Gulliver
Yahoo

Hamlet
William Shakespeare (1600)
Bernardo
Claudius
Fortinbras
Francisco
Gertrude
Guildenstern
Hamlet
Horatio
Ophelia
Rosencrantz

Hard Times
Charles Dickens (1854)
Bitzer
Gradgrind
Jupe
Kidderminster
Loo
M'Choakumchild
Sissy

Heartbreak House
Bernard Shaw (1917)
Addy
Lady Ariadne
Billy
Boss
Ellie
Hessy
Hector Hushabye
Mazzini
Randall
Captain Shotover

Henry VIII
William Shakespeare (1612)
Brandon
Duke of Norfolk
Duke of Buckingham
Earl of Surrey
Griffith
King Henry
Lord Chamberlain
Queen Katherine
Wolsey

Henry V
William Shakespeare (1598)
Bardolph
Henry
Pistol

Henry IV
William Shakespeare (1597)
Archibald
Doll
Fang
Henry
Hotspur
Morton
Page
Percy
Peto
Poins
Shadow
Snare
Travers

The House of the Seven Gables
Nathaniel Hawthorne (1851)
Clifford
Colonel
Hepzibah
Jaffrey

Huckleberry Finn
Mark Twain (1885)
- The Duke
- Granderford
- Huckleberry
- The King
- Polly
- Shepardson
- Widow

Horseman, Pass
Larry McMurtry (1961)
- Hud

The Hunchback of Notre Dame
Victor Hugo (1831)
- Claude
- Dauphin
- Esmeralda
- Gudule
- Jacques
- Pierre
- Quasimodo
- Tristan

The Idylls of the King
Alfred Lord Tennyson (1859)
- Balan
- Balin
- Bors
- Camelot
- Galahad
- Gareth
- Gawain
- Geraint
- Guinevere
- Kay
- King Arthur
- Lancelot
- Merlin
- Modred
- Morning Star
- Percivale
- Tristram
- Uther

The Iliad
Homer (c. Tenth Century B.C.)
- Achilles
- Ajax
- Apollo
- Ares
- Athena
- Dolon
- Heben
- Hector
- Hecuba
- Hera
- Nestor
- Odysseus
- Paris
- Poseidon
- Priam
- Teucer
- Zeus

The Invisible Man
H.G. Wells (1897)
- Griffin
- Marvel

Jude the Obscure
Thomas Hardy (1895)
- Jude

Julius Caesar
William Shakespeare (1599)
- Anthony
- Brutus
- Caesar
- Calpurnia
- Cassius
- Julius
- Lucius
- Marcus
- Strato
- Titinius

The Jungle Books
Rudyard Kipling (1894-95)
  Akela
  Bagheera
  Baloo
  Buldeo
  Mowgli
  Shere Khan
  Wolf

King John
William Shakespeare (1594)
  Chatillion
  Constance
  Hubert
  King John
  Lady
  Queen Elinor

King Lear
William Shakespeare (1605)
  Cordelia
  Edgar
  Edmund
  Goneril
  Lear
  Oswald
  Regan

Lady Chatterley's Lover
D.H. Lawrence (1928)
  Lady Chatterley

The Last of the Mohicans
James Fenimore Cooper (1826)
  Colonel Munro
  Hawkeye
  Major Duncan
  Marquis de Montcalm
  Natty Bumppo
  Uncas

The Legend of Sleepy Hollow
Washington Irving (1819)
  Gunpowder
  Ichabod
  Katrina

Little Dorrit
Charles Dickens (1855)
  Bangham
  Casby
  Clarance
  Dorrit
  Fanny
  Ferdinand
  Jeremiah
  Junior
  Maggy
  Meagles

Macbeth
William Shakespeare (1606)
  Donalbain
  Duncan
  Hecate
  Lennox
  Macbeth
  Macduff
  Malcolm
  Ross

The Maltese Falcon
Dashiell Hammett (1930)
  Archer
  Brigid
  Casper
  Effie
  Jacobi
  Spade
  Thursby
  Wilmer

Martin Chuzzlewit
Charles Dickens (1843)
  Bailey
  Charity
  Cherry
  Chevy
  Chuffey
  Chuzzlewit
  Crimple
  Fips
  Jinkins
  Jobling
  Lewsome
  Mercy
  Merry
  Montague
  Pip
  Spottletoe

Measure for Measure
William Shakespeare (1604)
  Angelo
  Barnardine
  Claudio
  Elbow
  Froth
  Isabella
  Lucio
  Pompey
  Provost
  Vincentio

The Merchant of Venice
William Shakespeare (1596)
  Antonio
  Bassanio
  Lancelot
  Old Gobbo
  Shylock
  Tubal

A Midsummer Night's Dream
William Shakespeare (1595)
  Demetrius
  Helena
  Hermia
  Hippolyta
  Lysander
  Oberon
  Puck
  Quince
  Snout
  Snug
  Theseus
  Titania

Mister Roberts
Thomas Heggen (1946)
  Captain Morton
  Chief Dowdy
  Doc
  Mister Roberts

Moby Dick
Herman Melville (1851)
  Captain Ahab
  Bulkington
  Elijah
  Fedallah
  Flask
  Fleece
  Ishmael
  King-Post
  Moby Dick
  Paggoo
  Perth
  Pip
  Starbuck
  Stubb

Mutiny on the Bounty
Charles Nordhoff and James N. Hall (1932)
  Captain Bligh
  Fletcher

Morrison
Muspratt
Peggy
Tehani
Tinkler

Nicholas Nickleby
Charles Dickens (1838)
Bolder
Cheeryble
Cobbey
Gregsby
Mulberry
Nicholas Nickleby
Pyke
Smike
Wackford Squeers

The Odyssey
Homer (c. Tenth Century B.C.)
Athena
Caertes
Calypso
Circe
Nestor
Odysseus
Penelope

Of Mice and Men
John Steinbeck (1937)
Candy
Crooks
Curley
Lennie Small
Slim

The Old Curiosity Shop
Charles Dickens (1840)
Abel
Cheggs
Chuckster
Dick
Jiniwin
Kit

Little Nell
Nibbles
Wackles

Oliver Twist
Charles Dickens (1837)
Artful Dodger
Brownlow
Bumble
Fagin
Fang
Maylie
Oliver

Othello
William Shakespeare (1604)
Bianca
Montano
Othello

Paul Bunyan
James Stevens (1925)
Babe
Bunyan
Helson
Johnny
King Bourbon
Niagara
Shanty Boy

Peter Pan
James M. Barrie (1904)
Darling
Captain Hook
Nana
Nibs
Peter Pan
Slightly
Smee
Tinker Bell
Tooties

The Rape of the Lock
Alexander Pope (1712)
   Ariel
   Belinda
   Clarissa
   Sir Plume
   Shock
   Spleen

Richard II
William Shakespeare (1595)
   Abbot
   Bagot
   Berkeley
   Bushy
   Duchess of York
   Hotspur
   King Richard
   Langley

Rip Van Winkle
Washington Irving (1819)
   Hudson
   Rip
   Wolf

Robin Hood
Unknown (1490)
   Friar Tuck
   King John
   Little John
   Maid Marian
   Robin Hood
   Scarlet

Robinson Crusoe
Daniel Defoe (1719)
   Friday
   Robinson Crusoe

Romeo and Juliet
William Shakespeare (1594)
   Benvolio
   Capulet

Friar John
Juliet
Mercutio
Montague
Romeo
Sampson

Silas Marner
George Eliot (1861)
   Godfrey Cass
   Squire Cass
   Dolly
   Dunsey
   Dunstan
   Eppie
   Silas Marner
   Molly
   Winthrop

The Sound and the Fury
William Faulkner (1929)
   Bascomb
   Benjy
   Caddy
   Compson
   Dilsey
   Frony
   Luster
   Quentin
   T.P.

The Taming of the Shrew
William Shakespeare (1596)
   Baptista
   Bianca
   Curtis
   Grumio
   Katherina
   Lucentio
   Petruchio
   Tranio

The Tempest
William Shakespeare (1611)
  Alonso
  Antonio
  Ariel
  Caliban
  Ferdinand
  Gonzalo
  Miranda
  Prospero
  Sebastian
  Stephano
  Trinculo

Tess of the D'Urbervilles
Thomas Hardy (1891)
  Angel
  Car Darch
  Derbyfield
  Felix
  Izz Huett
  Sorrow
  Tess

The Three Musketeers
Alexandre Dumas (1844)
  Aramis (Musketeer)
  Athos (Musketeer)
  D'Artagnan
  DeTreville
  Milady
  Porthos (Musketeer)

To Kill a Mockingbird
Harper Lee (1960)
  Atticus
  Boo
  Dill
  Jem
  Scout

Tom Sawyer
Mark Twain (1876)
  Becky

  Huckleberry Finn
  Injun Joe
  Muff
  Polly
  Tom Sawyer
  Sid

Treasure Island
Robert Louis Stevenson (1883)
  Black Dog
  Bill Bones
  Captain
  Ben Gunn
  Hands
  Jim Hawkins
  Long John
  Squire

Ulysses
James Joyce (1922)
  Armstrong
  Blazes
  Buck
  Cochrane
  Coffey
  Deasy
  Gertie
  Kinch
  Milly
  Molly
  Paddy
  Talbot

Uncle Tom's Cabin
Harriet Beecher Stowe (1852)
  Cassy
  Eliza
  Emmeline
  Haley
  Harry
  Shelby
  Simon
  Uncle Tom
  Topsy

116

Vanity Fair
William Makepeace Thackeray
  (1847)
  Becky
  Mrs. Bent
  Briggs
  Dobbin
  Dolly
  Georgy
  Horrocks
  Jos
  Osborne
  Sir Pitt
  Polly
  Rawdon
  Mr. Smee
  Lord Steyne
  Stubble
  Tinker
  Tufto
  Wirt

War and Peace
Count Leo Tolstoy (1866)
  Boris
  Helene
  Natasha
  Nikolay
  Pierre
  Rostov
  Sonya
  Vasily

Winesburg, Ohio
Sherwood Anderson (1919)
  Bentley
  Wing Biddlebaum
  Reefy
  Swift
  Willard

Wuthering Heights
Emily Brontë (1848)
  Heathcliff
  Hindley
  Linton
  Zillah

The Yearling
Marjorie K. Rawlings (1938)
  Arch
  Buck
  Flag
  Fodder-wing
  Gabby
  Hutto
  Jody
  Nellie
  Penny
  Slewfoot
  Twink

"Charlie Chan"

25

Memorable Characters from the Movies

AND now for you movie buffs, here are some memorable characters from the silver screen whom you may want to name your dog after. As in the preceding chapter, we can't include everyone's favorite, but this selection will get you off to a good start. (You will notice that most of our choices of movies are oldies but goodies.) In addition to the movie character's name, the actor or actress who played the role is also given.

The African Queen (1951)
      Charlie Allnut/*Humphrey Bogart*
      Rose Sayer/*Katharine Hepburn*

All About Eve (1950)
      Margo Channing/*Bette Davis*
      Eve Harrington/*Anne Baxter*
      Addison DeWitt/*George Sanders*
      Birdie/*Thelma Ritter*

All Quiet on the Western Front (1930)
> Baumer/*Lew Ayers*
> Katczinsky/*Louis Wolheim*
> Leer/*Scott Kolk*
> Duval/*Raymond Griffith*

All the King's Men (1949)
> Willie Stark/*Broderick Crawford*
> Tom Stark/*John Ireland*
> Sadie Burke/*Mercedes McCambridge*

All This and Heaven Too (1940)
> Henriette/*Bette Davis*
> Duc De Praslin/*Charles Boyer*

An American in Paris (1951)
> Mulligan/*Gene Kelly*
> Lise/*Leslie Caron*

Anastasia (1956)
> Anastasia/*Ingrid Bergman*
> Prince/*Yul Brynner*

Anchors Away (1945)
> Brady/*Gene Kelly*
> Clarence Doolittle/*Frank Sinatra*
> Carlos/*Carlos Ramirez*

Angels with Dirty Faces (1938)
> Frazier/*Humphrey Bogart*
> Laury Ferguson/*Ann Sheridan*
> Mac Keefer/*George Bancroft*
> Soapy/*Billy Halop*
> Swing/*Bobby Jordan*
> Bim/*Leo Gorcey*

Animal Crackers (1930)
> Capt. Geoffrey F. Spaulding/*Groucho Marx*
> The Professor/*Harpo Marx*
> Emanuel Ravelli/*Chico Marx*
> Horatio W. Jamison/*Zeppo Marx*

Anna and the King of Siam (1946)
Anna/*Irene Dunne*
The King/*Rex Harrison*
Tuptim/*Linda Darnell*

Anna Christie (1930)
Anna Christie/*Greta Garbo*
Matt Burke/*Charles Bickford*

Annie Get Your Gun (1950)
Annie Oakley/*Betty Hutton*
Buffalo Bill/*Louis Calhern*
Sitting Bull/*J. Carrol Naish*
Pawnee Bill/*Edward Arnold*

Another Thin Man (1938)
Nick Charles/*William Powell*
Nora Charles/*Myrna Loy*
Nicky/*William A. Poulson*
Asta/*Asta*
Dum Dum/*Abner Biberman*

Around the World in 80 Days (1956)
Phileas Fogg/*David Niven*
Passepartout/*Cantinflas*
Mr. Fix/*Robert Newton*
Aouda/*Shirley MacLaine*

Arsenic and Old Lace (1944)
Mortimer Brewster/*Cary Grant*
O'Hara/*Jack Carson*

As You Desire Me (1932)
Zara/*Greta Garbo*
Bruno/*Melvin Douglas*
Salter/*Erich Von Stroheim*

Auntie Mame (1958)
Auntie Mame/*Rosalind Russell*
Beauregard Burnside/*Forrest Tucker*

Babes in Arms (1939)
Mickey Moran/*Mickey Rooney*
Patsy Barton/*Judy Garland*

Barefoot in the Park (1967)

Paul Bratter/*Robert Redford*
Corie Bratter/*Jane Fonda*
Victor Velasco/*Charles Boyer*

Ben Hur (1959)

Ben Hur/*Charlton Heston*
Quintus Arrius/*Jack Hawkins*
Esther/*Haya Harareet*
Messala/*Stephen Boyd*

Bonnie and Clyde (1967)

Clyde/*Warren Beatty*
Bonnie/*Faye Dunaway*
Buck Barrow/*Gene Hackman*

Boys' Town (1938)

Father Flanagan/*Spencer Tracy*
Whitey Marsh/*Mickey Rooney*
Butch/*Wesley Giraud*

The Caine Mutiny (1954)

Captain Queeg/*Humphrey Bogart*
Lt. Barney Greenwald/*José Ferrer*

Casablanca (1942)

Rick Blaine/*Humphrey Bogart*
Ilsa Lund Laszlo/*Ingrid Bergman*
Captain Louis Renault/*Claude Rains*

Cat on a Hot Tin Roof (1958)

Maggie/*Elizabeth Taylor*
Brick/*Paul Newman*
Big Daddy/*Burl Ives*
Big Mama/*Judith Anderson*
Gooper/*Jack Carson*

The Champ (1931)

Champ/*Wallace Beery*
Pink/*Jackie Cooper*

Citizen Kane (1941)

Kane/*Orson Welles*
Jedediah Leland/*Joseph Cotten*

Dial M for Murder (1954)
>Tony/*Ray Milland*
>Margot/*Grace Kelly*

Doctor Doolittle (1967)
>Doctor Doolittle/*Rex Harrison*
>Emma Fairfax/*Samantha Eggar*
>Matthew Mugg/*Anthony Newley*

Dr. No (1962)
>James Bond 007/*Sean Connery*
>Felix Leiter/*Jack Lord*
>Dr. No/*Joseph Wiseman*
>Honey Ryder/*Ursula Andress*
>Monypenny/*Lois Maxwell*

Doctor Zhivago (1965)
>Tonya/*Geraldine Chaplin*
>Lara/*Julie Christie*
>Yuri/*Omar Sharif*

Gentlemen Prefer Blondes (1953)
>Dorothy/*Jane Russell*
>Lorelei/*Marilyn Monroe*

Gigi (1958)
>Gigi/*Leslie Caron*
>Lachaille/*Maurice Chevalier*

Going My Way (1944)
>Father O'Malley/*Bing Crosby*
>Genevieve Linden/*Risë Stevens*
>Father Fitzgibbon/*Barry Fitzgerald*

Gone with the Wind (1939)
>Scarlett O'Hara/*Vivien Leigh*
>Ashley Wilkes/*Leslie Howard*
>Rhett Butler/*Clark Gable*
>Mammy/*Hattie McDaniel*

The Greatest Show on Earth (1952)
>Holly/*Betty Hutton*
>Sebastian/*Cornel Wilde*
>Buttons/*James Stewart*
>Angel/*Gloria Grahame*

Guys and Dolls (1955)
>Sky Masterson/*Marlon Brando*
>Nathan Detroit/*Frank Sinatra*

High Noon (1952)
>Will Kane/*Gary Cooper*

High Society (1956)
>C.K. Dexter-Haven/*Bing Crosby*
>Tracy Lord/*Grace Kelly*
>Connor/*Frank Sinatra*

It Happened One Night (1934)
>Peter Warne/*Clark Gable*
>Ellie Andrews/*Claudette Colbert*
>Danker/*Alan Hale*

It's A Wonderful Life (1946)
>George Bailey/*James Stewart*
>Potter/*Lionel Barrymore*

Jailhouse Rock (1957)
>Vince Everett/*Elvis Presley*
>Hunk Houghton/*Mickey Shaughnessy*
>Teddy Talbot/*Dean Jones*

Key Largo (1948)
>McCloud/*Humphrey Bogart*
>Rocco/*Edward G. Robinson*
>Nora/*Lauren Bacall*
>Toots/*Harry Lewis*

Lawrence of Arabia (1962)
>T.E. Lawrence/*Peter O'Toole*
>Prince Feisal/*Alec Guinness*
>Auda abu Tayi/*Anthony Quinn*

Life with Father (1947)
>Clarence/*William Powell*
>Vinnie/*Irene Dunne*

The Maltese Falcon (1941)
>Sam Spade/*Humphrey Bogart*
>Brigid O'Shaughnessy/*Mary Astor*

The Mark of Zorro (1940)
>Diego Vega/*Tyrone Power*
>Lolita Quintero/*Linda Darnell*

Mary Poppins (1964)
>Mary Poppins/*Julie Andrews*
>Bert/Old Dawes/*Dick Van Dyke*

Meet Me in St. Louis (1944)
>Esther Smith/*Judy Garland*
>Tootie Smith/*Margaret O'Brien*

A Midsummer Night's Dream (1935)
>Bottom/*James Cagney*
>Lysander/*Dick Powell*
>Flute/*Joe E. Brown*
>Quince/*Frank McHugh*

Mister Roberts (1935)
>Lieutenant Doug Roberts/*Henry Fonda*
>The Captain/*James Cagney*
>Doc/*William Powell*

The Music Man (1961)
>Harold Hill/*Robert Preston*
>Marian Paroo/*Shirley Jones*
>Marcellus Washburn/*Buddy Hackett*
>Winthrop Paroo/*Ron Howard*

Mutiny on the Bounty (1935)
>Fletcher Christian/*Clark Gable*
>Captain Bligh/*Charles Laughton*
>Bachus/*Dudley Digges*
>Ellison/*Eddie Quillan*

National Velvet (1944)
>Velvet Brown/*Elizabeth Taylor*
>Mi Taylor/*Mickey Rooney*

Notorious (1946)
>Devlin/*Cary Grant*
>Alexander Sebastian/*Claude Rains*
>Alicia Huberman/*Ingrid Bergman*

Oklahoma (1955)
    Curley/*Gordon McRae*
    Ado Annie/*Gloria Grahame*
    Gertie/*Barbara Lawrence*

Old Yeller (1957)
    Coates/*Fess Parker*
    Travis/*Tommy Kirk*
    Old Yeller/*Spike (Dog)*

Porgy and Bess (1959)
    Porgy/*Sidney Poitier*
    Bess/*Dorothy Dandridge*
    Sportin' Life/*Sammy Davis, Jr.*
    Crown/*Brock Peters*
    Jake/*Leslie Scott*

Psycho (1960)
    Norman Bates/*Anthony Perkins*
    Marion Crane/*Janet Leigh*

Rio Bravo (1959)
    John T. Chance/*John Wayne*
    Dude/*Dean Martin*
    Colorado Ryan/*Ricky Nelson*
    Feathers/*Angie Dickinson*
    Stumpy/*Walter Brennan*

Sabrina (1954)
    Linus Larrabee/*Humphrey Bogart*
    Sabrina Fairchild/*Audrey Hepburn*

The Shaggy Dog (1959)
    Wilson Daniels/*Fred MacMurray*
    Wilby Daniels/*Tommy Kirk*
    Buzz Miller/*Tom Considine*
    Moochie Daniels/*Kevin Corcoran*

She Done Him Wrong (1933)
    Lady Lou/*Mae West*
    Captain Cummings/*Cary Grant*

Singin' in the Rain (1952)
    Lockwood/*Gene Kelly*
    Cosmo Brown/*Donald O'Connor*

Some Like It Hot (1959)
> Sugar Kane/*Marilyn Monroe*
> Joe/*Tony Curtis*
> Daphne/*Jack Lemmon*
> Spats Columbo/*George Raft*

South Pacific (1958)
> Nellie Forbush/*Mitzi Gaynor*
> Luther Billis/*Ray Walston*
> Emile De Becque/*Rossano Brazzi*
> Bloody Mary/*Juanita Hall*

Spellbound (1945)
> Constance Peterson/*Ingrid Bergman*
> J.B./*Gregory Peck*
> Harry/*Donald Curtis*

Splendor in the Grass (1961)
> Wilma Dean/*Natalie Wood*
> Bud Stamper/*Warren Betty*

Stagecoach (1939)
> Ringo Kid/*John Wayne*
> Dallas/*Claire Trevor*
> Curley/*George Bancroft*
> Buck/*Andy Devine*

Take Me Out to the Ball Game (1949)
> Ryan/*Frank Sinatra*
> K.C. Higgins/*Esther Williams*
> Eddie O'Brien/*Gene Kelly*

Thoroughly Modern Milly (1967)
> Millie Dillmount/*Julie Andrews*
> Muzzy Van Hossmere/*Carol Channing*
> Cruncher/*Lou Nova*

Top Hat (1935)
> Jerry Travers/*Fred Astaire*
> Dale Tremont/*Ginger Rogers*

Wee Willie Winkie (1937)
>Priscilla Williams/*Shirley Temple*
>Coppy/*Michael Whalen*
>Khoda Khan/*Cesar Romero*
>Bagby/*Brandon Hurst*

West Side Story (1961)
>Maria/*Natalie Wood*
>Tony/*Richard Beymer*
>Riff/*Russ Tamblyn*

When My Baby Smiles At Me (1948)
>Bonny/*Betty Grable*
>Skid/*Dan Dailey*
>Bozo/*Jack Oakie*
>Gussie/*June Havoc*

The Wizard of Oz (1939)
>Dorothy/*Judy Garland*
>The Wizard/*Frank Morgan*
>Hank (Scarecrow)/*Ray Bolger*
>Zeke (Cowardly Lion)/*Bert Lahr*
>Hickory (Tin Woodman)/*Jack Haley*
>Glinda/*Billie Burke*
>Toto/*Toto*
>The Wicked Witch/*Margaret Hamilton*

26

Famous Dogs

HERE'S a list of some famous dogs in their own right. Some are real, some fictional:

Argus In Homer's *Odyssey*, the hound who recognized the voice and footsteps of his master, Odysseus, who returned from the Trojan Wars disguised as a beggar. Only Argus was able to recognize Odysseus upon his return to Ithaca after so many years.

Asta The Wire Fox Terrier who starred in the *Thin Man* series with William Powell and Myrna Loy.

Balto The dog that, in a blizzard, led a sled carrying diphtheria serum to Nome, Alaska during a 1925 epidemic.

Batka The German Shepherd who was the main character in Romain Gary's book *White Dog*.

Beau General Omar Bradley's famous Poodle.

Belle Arthur Treacher's Yorkshire Terrier.

Benji	The main character in the movie *Benji*.
Blemie	The Dalmatian owned by playwright Eugene O'Neill.
Boatswain	The Newfoundland owned by Lord Byron.
Bob	The Scots Guards' black and white terrier that served as the regiment's mascot during part of the nineteenth century.
Buck	The main character in Jack London's great novel *The Call of the Wild*.
Buddy	The first seeing eye dog in the United States, 1928.
Bullet	Roy Roger's German Shepherd, who, after he died, was stuffed and displayed together with the cowboy's horse Trigger.
Bull's-eye	The name of Bill Sikes' Bull Terrier in *Oliver Twist*, by Charles Dickens.
Caesar	The dog owned by poet Robert Burns.
Cavall	The legendary hound owned by King Arthur.
Charley	The Poodle owned by playwright John Steinbeck, who was also the hero of Steinbeck's book, *Travels with Charley*.
Chesapeake	The Chesapeake Bay Retriever is the official state dog of Maryland.
Chips	First United States sentry dog that was sent overseas during World War II who was awarded the Purple Heart and also the Silver Star.
Cleo	The Basset Hound who starred in the television series *The People's Choice*.
Cristabel, Feely, Jennie, Josephine, Julie, Sophie and Tessa	Novelist James Thurber's pet dogs.

130

Coll	The dog owned by famous poet Chaucer.
Crab	This dog appeared in *The Two Gentlemen of Verona* and was the only dog ever in a Shakespearean play.
Dake	The first Scottish Terrier registered in the United States.
Dart and Music	The Greyhounds owned by poet William Wadsworth.
Dick	The dog who served as the mascot for the U.S.S. Constitution ("Old Ironsides").
Fido	Abraham Lincoln's sons Willie and Tad owned this shaggy brown dog. The year following the President's assassination, Fido was killed by a frightened drunk whom the dog had playfully attacked.
Flossie and Keeper	The spaniel owned by Anne Bronte and the Bullmastiff owned by her sister Emily.
Jo-Fi	The Chow Chow owned by Sigmund Freud.
Lad	Albert Payson Terhune's Collie, who was the hero in many of the author's books.
Lady	A dog owned by George Washington.
Lassie	The famous Collie who was the main character in Eric Knight's 1938 short story of that name. In 1941, MGM bought the movie rights for $100,000.
Marco	Queen Victoria of England's Pomeranian.
Max	The bionic German Shepherd who costarred with Lindsay Wagner in "The Bionic Woman" television series.
Mike	The Border Collie that stars in the movie *Down and Out in Beverly Hills*. His distinguishing characteristic is his one blue and one brown eye.

Monsieur de Niagra   The first messenger dog in North America.

Mopsey   A dog owned by George Washington.

Mushka   A dog sent into space by the Russians on an early flight.

Neil   The Saint Bernard ghost who drinks martinis in the "Topper" television series.

Old Yeller   The Yellow Labrador Retriever in the movie *Old Yeller.*

Pat   The dog in the children's story, *Hop on Pop,* by Dr. Seuss.

Peng   A dog who was trained to be a co-pilot in the Israeli Air Force.

Pete   The dog who appeared in the *Our Gang* movies.

Pluto   The famous character who was featured in Walt Disney cartoons. Pluto has the ears of a Bloodhound, the tail of an Irish Water Spaniel, and the nose of Rudolph, the Red-Nosed Reindeer.

Ralph   The dog in the book by Walter Lorraine entitled *The Dog Who Thought He was a Boy.*

Rin Tin Tin   The famous German Shepherd who starred in many movies of the 1920s.

Scannon   A black Newfoundland belonging to Meriwether Lewis who acted as a watchdog during the Lewis and Clark exploration of the Missouri River.

Scraps   Charlie Chaplin's pet dog in the film "A Dog's Life."

Shep   A fictional Collie who tended sheep in Central Park in New York, N.Y. in the early twentieth century.

Smokey   A dog who served as the mascot for the University of Tennessee's football team in the late 1960s.

Snoopy   The famous comic strip Beagle who is featured in Charles Shultz's *Peanuts.*

Stonewall   A black-and-white dog who served as the mascot for a regiment from Richmond, Virginia during the Civil War.

Tiger   The family pet owned by the Brady Family in the television series "The Brady Bunch."

Toto   The Cairn Terrier in *The Wizard of Oz.*

Tramp   The household pet owned by the Douglas family in the television series "My Three Sons."

Yukon King   The sled dog who starred in the television series "Sergeant Preston of the Yukon."

"Ike"

27

Birthday Dogs

HOW about naming your dog after somebody born on the same day as him or her—or on the date that you first received your puppy? Here's a list of famous people and their birthdays for every day of the year:

January
1   Barry Goldwater, U.S. senator; Rocky Graziano, boxer; J. Edgar Hoover, FBI chief; Paul Revere, patriot; J.D. Salinger, author.
2   Isaac Asimov, author; Bill Bradley, basketball player/U.S. senator; Julius LaRosa, singer; Bill Madlock, baseball player.
3   Dabney Coleman, actor; Bobby Hull, hockey player; Zasu Pitts, actress.
4   Louis Braille, teacher of the blind; Jane Wyman, actress.
5   Robert Duvall, actor; Diane Keaton, actress; Walter "Fritz" Mondale, former Vice President.
6   Joan of Arc, heroine; Carl Sandburg, poet.
7   Alvin Dark, baseball player; Babe Pratt, hockey player.
8   David Bowie, singer; Little Anthony, singer; Elvis Presley, singer; Soupy Sales, comedian.
9   Joan Baez, singer; Crystal Gayle, singer; Gypsy Rose Lee, actress; Richard Nixon, former President; Bart Starr, football player.
10 Ethan Allen, revolutionary; Ray Bolger, actor; Frank Sinatra, singer; Walter Travis, golfer.

11 General Crowder, baseball player; Red Hamill, hockey player; Rod Taylor, actor.
12 Joe Frazier, boxer; Jack London, author; Mac Speedie, football player.
13 Horatio Alger, author; Charles Nelson Reilly, actor.
14 Benedict Arnold, soldier; Faye Dunaway, actress; Albert Schweitzer, humanitarian.
15 Lloyd Bridges, actor; Martin Luther King, Jr., civil rights leader.
16 Dizzy Dean, baseball player; Harry Carey, actor; Ethel Merman, singer.
17 Muhammad Ali, boxer; Al Capone, gangster; Anton Chekhov, playwright.
18 Oliver Hardy, actor; Danny Kaye, actor; Pedro Rodriguez, auto racer.
19 Janis Joplin, singer; Dolly Parton, singer; Edgar Allan Poe, poet.
20 George Burns, actor; Federico Fellini, director; Aristotle Onassis, shipping magnate.
21 Mac Davis, singer; Stonewall Jackson, military officer; Jack Nicklas, golfer; Telly Savalas, actor.
22 Francis Bacon, philosopher; D. W. Griffith, politician.
23 John Hancock, statesman; Jerry Tubbs, football player.
24 John Belushi, actor; Ernest Borgnine, actor.
25 Robert Burns, poet; Lou Groza, football player; Virginia Woolf, author.
26 Paul Newman, actor; Jack Youngblood, football player.
27 Mikhail Baryshnikov, dancer; Lewis Carroll, author; Troy Donahue, actor; Wolfgang Amadeus Mozart, composer.
28 Alan Alda, actor; Susan Sontag, author.
29 Owen Davis, playwright; William McKinley, President; Don Morrow, TV host.
30 Gene Hackman, actor; Hal Prince, director; Franklin D. Roosevelt, President.
31 Norman Mailer, author; Nolan Ryan, baseball player; Jackie Robinson, baseball player.

February
1 Clark Gable, actor; Garrett Morris, actor.
2 Farrah Fawcett-Major, actress.
3 Joey Bishop, comedian; Morgan Fairchild, actress; James Michener, author; Norman Rockwell, artist; Fran Tarkenton, football player.
4 Alice Cooper, singer; Charles Lindberg, aviator; Byron Nelson, golfer.

136

5   Hank Aaron, baseball player; Red Buttons, actor; Felix Mendelssohn, composer.

6   Tom Brokaw, newscaster; Fabian, singer; Christopher Marlowe, poet; Babe Ruth, baseball player.

7   Charles Dickens, author; Sinclair Lewis, author.

8   Nick Nolte, actor; William Sherman, army officer; Jules Verne, author.

9   Mia Farrow, actress; Carmen Miranda, singer; Roger Mudd, newscaster.

10 Jimmy Durante, comedian; Robert Wagner, actor.

11 Farouk I, King of Egypt; Eva Gabor, actress; Burt Reynolds, actor.

12 Abraham Lincoln, President; Joe Garagiola, baseball player; Lorne Greene, actor; Franco Zeffirelli, director.

13 Tennessee Ernie Ford, singer; Jean Muir, actress; Bess Truman, First Lady.

14 Jack Benny, comedian; Hugh Downs, TV host; JoJo Starbuck, ice skater.

15 Susan B. Anthony, reformer; Harvey Korman, actor; Cesar Romero, actor.

16 Edgar Bergen, ventriloquist; Sonny Bono, actor; John McEnroe, tennis player.

17 Ike Boone, baseball player; Montgomery Ward, merchant.

18 Enzo Ferrari, auto racer; James Goodrich, politician; Wendell Willkie, politician; Yoko Ono, artist; John Travolta, actor.

19 Lee Marvin, actor; Smokey Robinson, singer.

20 Sandy Duncan, actress; Patty Hearst, heiress; Gloria Vanderbilt, heiress.

21 Erma Bombeck, writer; Barbara Jordan, politician; Tom Tracy, football player.

22 Julius Erving, basketball player; Ted Kennedy, politician; George Washington, first President.

23 Peter Fonda, actor; George Handel, composer; Jim Youngblood, football player.

24 James Farentino, actor; Winslow Homer, artist.

25 Zeppo Marx, actor; Pierre Auguste Renoir, artist; Bobby Riggs, tennis player.

26 Johnny Cash, singer; Fats Domino, singer; Victor Hugo, author.

27 Joan Bennett, actress; Irwin Shaw, author; Elizabeth Taylor, actress.

28 Mario Andretti, auto racer; Vincente Minelli, director; Tommy Tune, dancer.

29 Jimmy Dorsey, musician; Alex Rocco, actor.

March

1 Harry Belafonte, singer; Robert Conrad, actor; Glenn Miller, musician.

2 Desi Arnaz, Sr., actor; Tom Wolfe, journalist.

3 Alexander Graham Bell, inventor; Jean Harlow, actress.

4 Buck Baker, auto racer; Theodore Giesel (Dr. Seuss), author; Charles Templeton, politician.

5 Jack Cassidy, actor; Rex Harrison, actor.

6 LeRoy Cooper, astronaut; Lou Costello, actor; Cyrano DeBergerac, poet; Michaelangelo, artist; Willie Stargell, baseball player.

7 Franco Harris, football player; Maurice Ravel, composer.

8 Oliver Wendell Holmes, jurist; Little Peggy March, singer.

9 Andy North, golfer; Arky Vaughan, baseball player.

10 Sandy Palmer, golfer; James Earl Ray, assassin.

11 Ralph Abernathy, civil rights leader; Torquato Tasso, poet; Lawrence Welk, musician.

12 Liza Minnelli, actress; Wally Shirra, astronaut.

13 Andy Bean, golfer; Tessie O'Shea, actress; Hugo Wolf, musician.

14 Michael Caine, actor; Billy Crystal, actor; Maxim Gorki, playwright; Quincy Jones, musician.

15 Beryl Carroll, politician; Andrew Jackson, President; Sabu, actor.

16 James Madison, President; Buddy Myer, baseball player; Hollis Stacy, golfer.

17 Nat King Cole, singer; Patrick Duffy, actor; Rudolf Nureyev, dancer.

18 Grover Cleveland, President; George Plimpton, author; Charley Pride, singer; Amerigo Vespucci, navigator.

19 Ursula Andress, actress; Wyatt Earp, gunfighter; Irving Wallace, author.

20 Bobby Orr, ice hockey player; Henrik Ibsen, playwright; Sir Michael Redgrave, actor.

21 Johann Sebastian Bach, composer; James Coco, actor; Florenz Ziegfeld, producer.

22 Orrin Hatch, politician; Chico Marx, actor; William Shatner, actor.

23 Hazel Dawn, actress; Moses Malone, basketball player.

24 Steve McQueen, actor; Larry Wilson, football player.

25 Hoyt Wayne Axton, singer; Aretha Franklin, singer; Elton John, singer.

26 Alan Arkin, actor; Leonard Nimoy, actor; Diana Ross, singer; Tennessee Williams, playwright.

27 Sarah Vaughn, singer; Michael York, actor.

28 Rick Barry, basketball player; Freddie Bartholomew, actor; August Anheuser Busch, Jr., brewing magnate.

29 Pearl Bailey, singer; Eugene McCarthy, politician; Cy Young, baseball player.

30 Warren Beatty, actor; Vincent Van Gogh, artist; Jerry Lucas, basketball player.

31 Herb Alpert, musician; Rene Descartes, philosopher; Sean O'Casey, playwright.

April

1 Lon Chaney, actor; Eddy Duchin, musician; Debby Reynolds, actress.

2 Buddy Ebsen, actor; Max Ernst, artist.

3 Doris Day, actress; Washington Irving, author; Wayne Newton, singer.

4 Rusty Staub, baseball player; Muddy Waters, singer.

5 Bette Davis, actress; Gregory Peck, actor; Spencer Tracy, actor; Booker T. Washington, educator.

6 Harry Houdini, magician; Billy Dee Williams, actor.

7 Francis Ford Coppola, director; Percy Faith, musician; Billie Holiday, singer; Robert L. Shook, author; William Wadsworth, poet.

8 Peggy Lennon, singer; Mary Pickford, actress.

9 Avery Schreiber, comedian; Efrem Zimbalist, musician.

10 Chuck Connors, actor; Nikolai Lenin, Russian politician; Omar Sharif, actor.

11 Joe Beauchamp, football player; Oleg Cassini, designer.

12 Henry Clay, statesman; Herbie Hancock, musician; Tiny Tim, singer.

13 Jim Barnes, basketball player; F. W. Woolworth, merchant.

14 Sir John Gielgud, actor; Pete Rose, baseball player; Rod Steiger, actor.

15 Leonardo da Vinci, artist; Robert Walker, actor.

16 Kareem Abdul-Jabbar, basketball player; Henry Mancini, musician.

17 Genevieve, entertainer; Nikita Khrushehev, Soviet Prime Minister; J. P. Morgan, financier.

18 Nate Archibald, basketball player; Wendy Barrie, actress.

19 Don Adams, actor; Dudley Moore, comedian.

20 Joan Miro, artist; Ryan O'Neal, actor.

21 Queen Elizabeth, II; Anthony Quinn, actor.

22 Isabella I, Queen of Spain; Jack Nicholson, actor.

23 James Buchanan, President; Lee Majors, actor; Vladmir Nabokov, author; Shirley Temple, actress.

24 Shirley Maclaine, actress; Barbra Streisand, actress/singer.

25 Ella Fitzgerald, singer; Meadowlark Lemon, basketball player; Al Pacino, actor.
26 Ferdinand Delacroix, artist; David Hume, philosopher; Bobby Rydell, singer.
27 Ulysses S. Grant, President; Jack Klugman, actor.
28 Ann-Margaret, actress; Lionel Barrymore, actor.
29 William Randolph Hearst, publisher; Rafael Sabatini, author.
30 Juliana, Queen of Netherlands; Perry King, actor; Willie Nelson, singer.

May

1 Steve Cauthen, jockey; Glenn Ford, actor; Duke of Wellington.
2 Catherine the Great, Russian Empress; Bing Crosby, singer.
3 Niccolo Machiavelli, philosopher; Golda Meir, Israeli Prime Minister; Frankie Valli, singer.
4 Audrey Hepburn, actress; Jack Tobin, baseball player.
5 Karl Marx, socialist writer.
6 Sigmund Freud, founder of psychoanalysis; Rudolph Valentino, actor.
7 Toti Fields, commedienne; Johnny Unitas, football player; Peter Tchaikovsky, composer.
8 Oscar Hammerstein, composer; James Mitchum, actor; Roberto Rosselini, director; William H. Vanderbilt, railroad magnate.
9 Pancho Gonzales, tennis player; Mike Wallace, newscaster.
10 Fred Astaire, actor; David Selznick, producer; Nancy Walker, actress.
11 Irving Berlin, composer; Foster Brooks, comedian.
12 Burt Bacharach, composer; Yogi Berra, baseball player; Dolly Madison, First Lady.
13 Joe Louis, boxer; Walt Whitman, poet; Stevie Wonder, singer.
14 Bobby Darin, singer; Gabriel Fahrenheit, physicist.
15 George Brett, baseball player; Jasper Johns, artist.
16 Henry Fonda, actor; Liberace, pianist.
17 Dennis Hopper, actor; Ayatollah Khomeini, politician.
18 Frank Capra, director; Perry Como, singer; Reggie Jackson, baseball player.
19 Ho Chi Minh, President of North Vietnam; Malcolm X, Black Muslim leader.
20 Jimmy Stewart, actor; Constance Towers, singer.
21 Lola Lane, actress; Alexander Pope, poet; Leo Sayer, singer.
22 Michael Constantine, actor; Peter Nero, musician; Sir Laurence Olivier, actor.
23 Scatman Crothers, actor; Zack Wheat, baseball player.
24 Bob Dylan, singer; Queen Victoria.

25 Claude Akins, actor; Ralph Waldo Emerson, writer; Marshal Tito, Yugoslav President.

26 Al Jolson, actor; John Wayne, actor.

27 John Cheever, writer; Henry Kissinger, diplomat; Vincent Price, actor.

28 Gladys Knight, singer; Jim Thorpe, athlete.

29 Bob Hope, actor; John F. Kennedy, President; Al Unser, auto racer.

30 Mel Blanc, actor; Gayle Sayers, football player.

31 Clint Eastwood, actor; Joe Namath, football player; Norman Vincent Peale, clergyman; Carrie Shook, author.

June

1 Cleavon Little, actor; Jo Jo White, baseball player.

2 Hedda Hopper, actress; Jerry Mathers, actor.

3 Jefferson Davis, President of the Confederacy; Suzie Quatro, actress.

4 Sandra Haynie, golfer; Dennis Weaver, actor.

5 Andre Lacroix, hockey player; Pancho Villa, Mexican bandit.

6 Bjorn Borg, tennis player; Frances Starr, actress.

7 Nikki Giovanni, poet; Thurman Munson, baseball player.

8 Boz Scaggs, singer; Robert Schumann, composer; Frank Lloyd Wright, architect.

9 George Axelrod, playwright; Peter the Great, Russian Emperor; Cole Porter, musician.

10 F. Lee Bailey, attorney; Saul Bellow, writer; Judy Garland, actress.

11 Jacques-Yves Cousteau, marine explorer; Vince Lombardi, football player; Jackie Stewart, auto racer; Gene Wilder, actor.

12 Raul Castro, politician; Jim Nabors, actor.

13 Red Grange, football player; Paul Lynde, actor; William Yeats, poet.

14 Happy Day, hockey player, Burl Ives, actor; Harriet Beecher Stowe, author.

15 Janet Lennon, singer; Sinclair Weeks, politician.

16 Stan Laurel, actor; Len Small, politician.

17 Dean Martin, actor; Sumner Sewall, politician; Stringbean, actor.

18 Lou Brock, baseball player; Paul McCartney, singer; Blanche Sweet, actress.

19 Guy Lombardo, musician; Malcolm McDowell, actor; Blaise Pascal, mathematician.

20 Chet Atkins, musician; Errol Flynn, actor; Lillian Hellman, playwright.

21 Rockwell Kent, artist; Jean-Paul Sartre, writer; Martha Washington, First Lady.

22 Gower Champion, dancer; Kris Kristofferson, singer; Billy Wilder, director.

23   Josephine de Beauharnis, French Empress; Duke of Windsor.

24   Jack Dempsey, boxer; Rollie Hemsley, baseball player.

25   Al Beauchamp, football player; George Orwell, author; Carly Simon, singer.

26   Pearl Buck, author; Abner Doubleday, baseball inventor.

27   Bones Raleish, hockey player; Willie Young, football player.

28   Mel Brooks, actor; Henry VIII, King of England; Jean-Jacques Rousseau, writer.

29   Nelson Eddy, actor; Slim Pickens, actor; Dizzy Trout, baseball player.

30   Lena Horne, actress; Buddy Rich, musician.

July

1   Dan Aykroyd, actor; Olivia de Havilland, actress; George Sand, actor; Twyla Tharp, dancer.

2   Renee Lacoste, tennis player; Olav V, King of Norway; Chuck Stobbs, baseball player.

3   Betty Buckley, actress; Cully Dahlstrom, hockey player; Geraldo Rivera, TV host.

4   Louis Armstrong, musician; George M. Cohan, musician; Calvin Coolidge, President; Giuseppe Garibaldi, Italian patriot; Nathaniel Hawthorne, author; Ann Landers, journalist and twin sister Abigail Van Buren, journalist; Eva Marie Saint, actress; Neil Simon, playwright; Uncle Sam.

5   P. T. Barnum, showman; Jean Cocteau, artist; Georges Pompidou, French President.

6   Sebastian Cabot, actor; Nancy Reagan, First Lady; Otto Graham, football player; Andrei Gromyko, Soviet statesman; Merv Griffin, TV host; John Paul Jones, Naval officer; Maximilian, Mexican Emperor; Sylvester Stallone, actor.

7   Marc Chagall, artist; Doc Severinsen, musician; Ringo Starr, musician.

8   Steve Lawrence, singer; Nelson A. Rockefeller, vice-president; George Romney, politician.

9   Spike Jones, football player; Thomas Erby Kilby, politician; O. J. Simpson, football player.

10   Nick Adams, actor; John Calvin, religious reformer; James Whistler, artist.

11   John Quincy Adams, President; Yul Brynner, actor; Tab Hunter, actor; E. B. White, author.

12   Bill Cosby, actor; Milton Berle, actor; George Washington Carver, botanist; Oscar Hammerstein, musician; Henry David Thoreau, author; Andrew Wyeth, artist.

13 Charles Coody, golfer; Jack Kemp, politician; Mickey Walker, boxer.
14 Ingmar Bergman, director; John Chancellor, newscaster; Gerald Ford, President; Woody Guthrie, singer.
15 Ken Kercheval, actor; Rembrandt Van Rijn, artist; Jan-Michael Vincent, actor.
16 Ginger Rogers, actress; Barbara Stanwyck, actress.
17 James Cagney, actor; Diahann Carroll, actress; Phyllis Diller, actress; Art Linkletter, TV host.
18 Hume Cronyn, actor; Dion, singer; Red Skelton, actor.
19 Edgar Degas, artist; George Hamilton IV, actor; Illie Nastase, tennis player.
20 Lola Albright, actress; Wiley Rutledge, jurist; Natalie Wood, actress.
21 Don Knotts, actor; Cat Stevens, musician; Robin Williams, actor.
22 Orson Bean, actor; Oscar De La Renta, designer; Rose Kennedy, President's mother.
23 Bert Convy, TV host; Pee Wee Reese, baseball player; Arthur Treacher, actor.
24 Lynda Carter, Miss USA; Ruth Buzzi, comedienne; Vera, designer.
25 Thomas Eakins, artist; Whitey Lockman, baseball player.
26 Gracie Allen, actress; Mick Jagger, musician; Carl Jung, psychoanalyst; George Bernard Shaw, playwright; Vivian Vance, actress.
27 Peggy Fleming, ice skater.
28 Vida Blue, baseball player; Jacqueline Onassis, First Lady; Rudy Vallee, singer.
29 Clara Bow, actress; Benito Mussolini, Italian dictator.
30 Paul Anka, musician; Emily Jane Bronte, author; Henry Ford, auto manufacturer; Arnold Schwarzenegger, actor.
31 Evonne Goolagon, tennis player; George Liberace, musician.

August
1 Dom Deluise, actor; Jack Kramer, tennis player; Herman Melville, author; Yves St. Laurent, designer.
2 Carroll O'Connor, actor; Peter O'Toole, actor; Jack Warner, producer.
3 Tony Bennett, singer; Tim Mayotte, tennis player; Leon Uris, author.
4 Percy Shelley, poet; Tuck Stainback, baseball player.
5 John Huston, director; Robert Taylor, actor.
6 Lucille Ball, actress; Ed Snead, golfer; Andy Warhol, artist; Alfred Tennyson, poet.
7 Mata Hari, spy; B. J. Thomas, musician.
8 Connie Stevens, actress; Mel Tillis, musician; Esther Williams, actress.

9 John Dryden, poet; Rod Laver, tennis player; Ken Norton, boxer.
10 Eddie Fisher, singer; Herbert Hoover, President; Junior Samples, comedian.
11 Mike Douglas, TV host; Alex Haley, author.
12 George Hamilton, actor; Buck Owens, singer; Jane Wyatt, actress.
13 Ruz Castro, Cuban politician; Alfred Hitchcock, director; Don Ho, singer; Annie Oakley, markswoman.
14 Susan Saint James, actress; Dick Tiger, boxer.
15 Princess Anne, Great Britain; Napoleon Bonaparte, French emperor; Lawrence of Arabia, soldier; Sir Walter Scott, author.
16 Menachem Begin, Israeli Prime Minister; Eydie Gorme, singer; Leslie Ann Warren, actress.
17 Davy Crockett, frontiersman; Robert De Niro, actor; Mae West, actress.
18 Roberto Clemente, baseball player; Max Factor, cosmetics manufacturer; Robert Redford, actor; Caspar Weinberger, U.S. Defense Secretary; Shelly Winters, actress.
19 Coco Chanel, designer; Malcolm Forbes, publisher; Ogden Nash, poet; Orville Wright, aviator.
20 Graig Nettles, baseball player; Jacqueline Susann, author.
21 Count Basie, musician; Wilt Chamberlain, basketball player; Kenny Rogers, singer.
22 Denton Cooley, heart surgeon; Claude DeBussy, musician.
23 Barbara Eden, actress; Gene Kelly, actor; Oliver Hazard Perry, naval officer.
24 Gus Bodnar, hockey player; Preston Foster, actor.
25 Leonard Bernstein, musician; Sean Connery, actor; Monty Hall, TV host.
26 Sparky Adams, baseball player; Swede Savage, auto racer.
27 Samuel Goldwyn, movie producer; Martha Raye, actress; Tuesday Weld, actress.
28 Johann Wolfgang Goethe, writer; Donald O'Connor, actor; Lou Piniella, baseball manager.
29 Ingrid Bergman, actress; John Locke, philosopher.
30 Jean Claude Killy, skier; Fred MacMurray, actor.
31 James Coburn, actor; Buddy Hackett, author.

September

1 Rico Carty, baseball player; Englebert Humperdinck, singer; Lili Tomlin, actress.
2 Terry Bradshaw, football player; Jimmy Connors, tennis player; Linda Purl, actress.
3 Kitty Carlisle, actress; Alan Ladd, actor; Dixie Lee Ray, politician.

4   Mitzi Gaynor, actress; Dick York, actor.

5   Jesse James, outlaw; Louis XIV, King of France; Raquel Welch, actress.

6   Jane Curtain, actress; Marquis de Lafayette, French statesman.

7   Elizabeth I, Queen of England; Buddy Holly, musician; Grandma Moses, artist.

8   Sid Caesar, actor; Patsy Cline, singer.

9   Jimmy the Greek, oddsmaker; Cardinal Richelieu, French states-man; Cliff Robertson, actor; Colonel Harland Sanders, fast foods magnate; Leo Tolstoy, author.

10   Adele Astaire, dancer; Arnold Palmer, golfer; Margaret Trudeau, First Lady of Canada.

11   Bear Bryant, football player; O. Henry, author; Lola Falane, actress.

12   Maurice Chevalier, actor; Dickie Moore, actor; Jesse Owens, athlete.

13   Sherwood Anderson, author; Claudette Colbert, actress; Mel Tormé, singer.

14   Jack Hawkins, actor; Joey Heatherton, actress; Ivan Pavlov, physiologist.

15   Agatha Christie, author; Jackie Cooper, actor; James Fenimore Cooper, author; Jean Renoir, artist; William Howard Taft, President; Fay Wray, actress.

16   Lauren Bacall, actress; Peter Falk, actor; B B. King, singer; J. C. Penney, merchant.

17   Anne Bancroft, actress; J. Willard Marriot, hotel magnate; Roddy McDowall, actor.

18   Frankie Avalon, singer; Robert Blake, actor; Greta Garbo, actress.

19   Mama Cass, singer; Joe Morgan, baseball player; Twiggy, actress; Adam West, actor.

20   Red Auerbach, basketball coach; Sophia Loren, actress; Upton Sinclair, author.

21   Hamilton Jordan, politician; Bill Murray, actor; H. G. Wells, author.

22   Debby Boone, singer; John Houseman, actor; Erich Von Stroheim, actor.

23   Ray Charles, singer; Mickey Rooney, actor; Bruce Springsteen, singer.

24   F. Scott Fitzgerald, author; Jim Henson, puppeteer; Hunchy Huernschemeyer, football player.

25   Michael Douglas, actor; William Faulkner, author; Barbara Walters, TV host.

26   T. S. Eliot, poet; George Gershwin, composer; Jack LaLanne, physical fitness expert; Olivia Newton-John, singer; Pope Paul VI.

27   Sada Thompson, actress; Kathy Whitworth, golfer; Whit Wyatt, baseball player.

28 Brigitte Bardot, actress; Al Capp, cartoonist; Georges Clemenceau, French Premier; Ben E. King, musician.
29 Gene Autry, actor; Jerry Lee Lewis, singer.
30 Truman Capote, author; Johnny Mathis, singer; Marilyn McCoo, singer.

October

1 Julie Andrews, actress; Jimmy Carter, President; Walter Matthau, actor.
2 Bud Abbott, actor; Mohandas K. Gandi, Hindu political leader; Spanky MacFarland, actor; Groucho Marx, actor; Rex Reed, journalist.
3 Emily Post, etiquette authority; Gore Vidal, author.
4 Charlton Heston, actor; Buster Keaton, actor.
5 Chester Arthur, President; Allan Winden, actor.
6 Thor Heyerdahl, explorer; Carole Lombard, actress; Jack Sharkey, boxer.
7 Niels Bohr, atomic physicist; Elijah Muhammad, religious leader.
8 Chevy Chase, actor; Juan Domingo Peron, Argentine President; Eddie Rickenbacker, aviator.
9 John Lennon, musician; Alistair Sim, actor.
10 Adlai Stevenson, U.S. diplomat; Giuseppe Verdi, composer; Ben Vereen, actor.
11 Eleanor Roosevelt, First Lady; Dottie West, singer.
12 Sally Little, golfer; Luciano Pavarotti, singer; Joan Rivers, comedienne.
13 Art Garfunkel, singer; Yves Montand, actor; Nipsy Russell, actor; Margaret Thatcher, British Prime Minister.
14 E. E. Cummings, author; Dwight D. Eisenhower, President; Lillian Gish, actress; Ralph Lauren, designer.
15 John Kenneth Galbraith, economist; Frederich Nietzsche, philosopher.
16 Eugene O'Neill, playwright; Oscar Wilde, playwright.
17 Jimmy Breslin, journalist; Evel Knievel, daredevil; Pope John Paul I.
18 Chuck Berry, singer; Jesse Helms, politician; Pierre Trudeau, Canadian Prime Minister.
19 Peter Max, artist; John LeCarre, author.
20 Joyce Brothers, psychologist; Art Buchwald, journalist; Sir Christopher Wren, architect.
21 Samuel Coleridge, poet; Dizzy Gillespie, musician; Alfred Nobel, inventor.
22 Joan Fontaine, actress; Annette Funicello, actress; Franz Liszt, composer.

23 Johnny Carson, TV host; Pelé, soccer player.
24 Morgee Masters, golfer; Dame Thorndike, actress.
25 Minnie Pearl, actress; Pablo Picasso, artist; Helen Reddy, singer.
26 Jackie Coogan, actor; Shah of Iran; Leon Trotsky, Russian revolutionary.
27 Roy Lichtenstein, artist; Theodore Roosevelt, President.
28 James Cook, navigator; Dody Goodman, actress; Jonas Salk, physician.
29 Fanny Brice, actress; Melba Moore, singer.
30 John Adams, President; Nino Farina, auto racer; Grace Slick, singer; Ezra Pound, poet.
31 John Keats, poet; Bucko McDonald, hockey player; Jane Pauley, TV hostess; Dan Rather, newscaster.

November
1 James Kilpatrick, author; Tom Mack, football player.
2 Daniel Boone, frontiersman; Marie Antoinette, Queen of France; James Polk, President.
3 William Cullen Bryant, poet; Charles Bronson, actor; Lulu, singer.
4 Art Carney, actor; Walter Cronkite, newscaster; Dixie Lee, singer.
5 Vivien Leigh, actress; Tatum O'Neal, actress; Sam Shephard, playwright; Paul Simon, singer.
6 Sally Field, actress; Junior Langlois, hockey player.
7 Albert Camus, author; Al Hirt, musician; Joni Mitchell, singer.
8 Alain Delon, actor; Katharine Hepburn, actress.
9 Spiro Agnew, Vice President; Hedy Lamarr, actress; Sargent Shriver, politician.
10 Chester Aldrich, politician; Claude Rains, actor; Roy Scheider, actor.
11 Fyodor Dostoyevsky, author; George Patton, U.S. General; Kurt Vonnegut, Jr., author.
12 Nadia Comaneci, gymnast; Grace Kelly, Princess of Monaco.
13 Dack Rambo, actor; Robert Louis Stevenson, author.
14 Prince Charles, Great Britain; Mamie Eisenhower, First Lady; King Hussein I, Jordan; Barbara Hutton, heiress; Claude Monet, artist.
15 Edward Asner, actor; Georgia O'Keefe, artist.
16 Burgess Meredith, actor; John Phillip Sousa, composer; JoJo White, basketball player.
17 Rock Hudson, actor; Gordon Lightfoot, singer; Tom Seaver, baseball player.
18 Imogene Coca, actress; Linda Evans, actress; Alan Shepard, astronaut.
19 Tommy Dorsey, musician; Indira Gandhi, Indian Prime Minister; Calvin Klein, designer.

20 Alistair Cooke, journalist; Robert Kennedy, politician; Dick Smothers, comedian.
21 Goldie Hawn, actress; Rene La Salle, explorer; Jean Voltaire, author.
22 Hoagy Carmichael, actor; Rodney Dangerfield, comedian; Charles DeGaulle, French President; George Eliot, author; Charles Schultz, cartoonist.
23 Abigail Adams, First Lady; Billy the Kid, outlaw; Boris Karloff, actor; Harpo Marx, comedian; Franklin Pierce, President.
24 William F. Buckley, journalist; Scott Joplin, musician; Zachary Taylor, President; Toulouse Lautrec-Monfa, artist.
25 Joe DiMaggio, baseball player; Ricardo Montalban, actor.
26 Robert Goulet, actor; Rich Little, comedian; Tina Turner, singer.
27 Jimi Hendrix, singer; Cornelius Vanderbilt, capitalist.
28 Brooks Atkinson, journalist; Gary Hart, politician; Hope Lange, actress.
29 Louisa May Alcott, author; C. S. Lewis, author; Chuck Mangione, musician.
30 Sir Winston Churchill, British Prime Minister; Dick Clark, TV host; G. Gordon Liddy, politician; Mark Twain, author; Efrem Zimbalist, Jr., actor.

December

1 Woody Allen, director; Gilbert O'Sullivan, singer; Richard Pryor, actor.
2 Alexander Haig, politician; Georges Seurat, artist.
3 Joseph Conrad, author; Gilbert Stuart, artist; Andy Williams, singer.
4 Wink Martindale, TV host; Lillian Russell, actress.
5 George Custer, military officer; Walt Disney, producer; Strom Thurmond, politician; Martin Van Buren, President.
6 Ira Gershwin, composer; Agnes Moorehead, actress.
7 Johnny Bench, baseball player; Harry Chapin, musician.
8 Maxmilian Schell, actor; James Thurber, author; Eli Whitney, inventor.
9 Beau Bridges, actor; Kirk Douglas, actor; Douglas Fairbanks, Jr., actor; Red Foxx, actor; Tip O'Neill, politician.
10 Tommy Kirk, actor; Dorothy Lamour, actress.
11 Fiorello LaGuardia, politician; Rita Moreno, actress.
12 Bob Barker, TV host; Frank Sinatra, singer; Dionne Warwick, singer.
13 Mary Todd Lincoln, First Lady; Christopher Plummer, actor; Dick Van Dyke, actor; George Shultz, U.S. Secretary of State.

14 James Doolittle, Air Force Officer; Patty Duke, actress; Spike Jones, musician.
15 J. Paul Getty, oil magnate; Tim Conway, comedian.
16 Ludwig Van Beethoven, composer; David Ben-Gurion, Israeli Prime Minister; Leonid Brezhnev, Soviet government leader.
17 Arthur Fiedler, musician; Richard Long, actor.
18 Ty Cobb, baseball player; Paul Klee, artist; Saki, author; Baron Karl Weber, composer.
19 David Susskind, TV host; Cicely Tyson, actress; Reginald Vanderbilt, investor.
20 Skye Aubrey, actress; Irene Dunne, actress.
21 Benjamin Disraeli, Prime Minister; George Ball, politician; Phil Donahue, TV host; Jane Fonda, actress; Joseph Stalin, Soviet dictator; Kurt Waldheim, Austrian President.
22 Steve Garvey, baseball player; Frank Kellogg, politician.
23 Jose Greco, dancer; Vincent Sardi, Sr., restauranteur; Helmut Schmidt, German politician.
24 Howard Hughes, industrialist; Robert Joffrey, choreographer.
25 Clara Barton, organizer of the American Red Cross; Louis Chevrolet, auto manufacturer; Larry Csonka, football player; Conrad Hilton, hotel magnate; Little Richard, musician; Sir Isaac Newton, mathematician; Anwar Sadat, Egyptian President; Rod Serling, author; Dame Rebecca West, author.
26 George Dewey, naval officer; Mao Tse-Tung, Chairman, Chinese Communist party; Henry Miller, author.
27 Marlene Dietrich, actress; Louis Pasteur, chemist.
28 Lew Ayres, actor; Lou Jacobi, actor; Hildegarde Neff, actress; Johnny Otis, singer.
29 Pablo Casals, musician; Andrew Johnson, President; Jon Voight, actor.
30 Rudyard Kipling, author; Sandy Koufax, baseball player; Simon Guggenheim, financier.
31 Jacques Cartier, explorer; Charles Cornwallis, English Army officer; Anthony Hopkins, actor; Henri Matisse, artist.

The Miniature Pinscher is a big dog in a small package, and is nicknamed the "King of Toys." Most owners find it easy to give him a fitting title.

Many owners of Wire Fox Terriers find that the breed's energetic, friendly personality is the key to the right name for their pets.

28

Trivia Names

IN case you still haven't selected a name, here's some interesting trivia which may inspire you.

Alfred Arnold Great Britain's oldest bachelor who died at the reported age of 112 in 1941.

An-An The Moscow zoo's famous giant panda.

Andrea Doria The name of the ship that collided with the Swedish liner "Stockholm" on July 26, 1956.

Beulah The nickname of the buzzer on radio and TV's "Truth or Consequences."

Big Ben Big Ben is the bell in the clock tower of London's Houses of Parliament that rings on the hour. This bell, which weighs thirteen tons, was named after Sir Benjamin Hall, the Chief Commissioner of Works at the time it was installed, because of his own large size.

Bluey A Queensland Heeler from Australia who lived until the age of 29 years and 5 months—*the oldest dog to have ever lived!*

Boatswain The Newfoundland pet of Lord Byron.

Bobbie A Collie who was lost by his owners while on a vacation, and who found his home in Wolcott, Indiana after a 2,000 mile trip which took him six months.

Bright Path Jim Thorpe's Indian name.

Buck The part Saint Bernard—part Scotch Shepherd who is the main character in Jack London's *Call of the Wild.*

Cher Ami The World War I carrier pigeon that helped save the lost battalion in the Battle of the Argonne, October, 1918. The bird is enshrined at the Smithsonian Institution.

Cleo and Caesar The early stage names of Sonny and Cher.

Clipper Jacqueline Kennedy Onassis' German Shepherd presented to her by Joseph Kennedy.

Dandelion The origin of this name is the French "dent de leon," or "lion's tooth." The plant's jagged leaves do, in fact, resemble the teeth of a lion; several other European languages refer to the plant as the lion's teeth.

Derby The word "derby" is used to describe certain horse races, such as the Kentucky Derby. The original derby, pronounced "darby," is held at Epsom Downs in Surrey, England. This race was started by the twelfth Earl of Derby, an enthusiastic sportsman who lived in Epsom. His idea was successful, and in his honor, the race was named for him—the derby.

Dukes The slang term "dukes," meaning fists, has an odd origin. The Duke of Wellington had such a large nose that "Duke" became a synonym for "nose." Then, a man's fist became a "Duke buster." In time, the expression was shortened, and "Dukes" became another term for fists.

Emma Nutt The first female telephone operator, September 1, 1878.

Emperor Ming The merciless emperor of the universe and from the planet Mongo in the "Flash Gordon" comic strip.

Figaro The main character in "The Barber of Seville."

Highball This word was late nineteenth century slang when drinking glasses were called "balls." Tall glasses were used for whiskey and soda, and the drink came to be known as the highball.

Hippocrates The Father of Medicine, he was a Greek physician of approximately the 4th century B.C.

Kato Detective Clousseau's valet in the "Pink Panther" series.

Kojak The detective played by actor Aristotle "Telly" Savalas.

Knickers Dutch brick bakers called "knickerbockers" wore loose knee pants. Such breeches came to be known as "knickerbockers," which was later shortened to "knickers."

Leo MGM's trademark lion was employed by the studio since 1928, and was played throughout the years by three different lions.

Macintosh The popular raincoat bears the name of its inventor, Charles Macintosh, who was the first man to discover waterproof fabrics.

Mardi Gras Mardi Gras is a French term meaning "fat Tuesday." On this day it was the custom in France to parade a fattened ox through the streets of the city. Mardi Gras falls on the day before Lent, Shrove

Tuesday, and since Lent was a period of fasting, Mardi Gras was the last chance for feasting and general revelry until Easter.

Mata Hari   She was Germany's most famous spy during World War II.

Mikado   This term is generally used by westerners to describe the Japanese emperor, meaning literally, "honorable door."

My Little Chickadee   This is the 1940 film starring Mae West and W. C. Fields. The screenplay was written by Miss West.

Packy Ease   Bob Hope's stage name during an attempted career in amateur boxing.

Patsy   The name of the annual award presented to animal performers on the silver screen and also on television by the American Humane Association. Patsy is an acronym for Performing Animal Top Star of the Year and also Picture Animal Top Star of the Year. "Francis the Talking Mule" was the first recipient and received his award from the society's first emcee, Ronald Reagan.

Polly   A Labrador Retriever who served as a guide dog for her blind owner for over 13 years—the longest ever.

Rosebud   The last dying word of Citizen Kane, as portrayed in the film by Orson Welles. Rosebud was the name of the brand of sled that Kane lost as a child, and the name became the frame of the theme of the film, as the story was told through the search for the word's meaning.

Rover   The code name for President Franklin Roosevelt's wife during World War II.

Runnymede   The meadow, along the River Thames, upon which the Magna Carta was signed on June 15, 1215 by King John.

St. Valentine   St. Valentine was a Roman priest who helped rescue early Christian martyrs. For this he was put in jail and finally clubbed to death. The day of his death fell on the day known as the "feast of the birds," the day in which it was believed that birds chose their mates for the coming year. Because of the romantic association, Valentine's Day became the day when lovers exchange tokens of affection.

Speedwell   A ship that was not seaworthy enough to accompany the "Mayflower" in 1620.

Taliaferro   Booker T. Washington's middle name (pronounced Tolliver). He was the first black person to be portrayed on a U.S. postage stamp (the 1940 ten-cent stamp).

Teddy   The "Teddy Bear" became popular when President Theodore Roosevelt caught a baby bear during a hunting expedition. A newspaper cartoon publicized the incident and captioned the drawing: "Teddy's Bear."

Traveler   Robert E. Lee's horse.

Yuri Gagarin   The first man in space on board the Russian Volstok 1, on April 12, 1961. He was in space for 1 hour and 48 minutes.

153

Vanilla   The dog on radio's "Amos 'n' Andy" series.

Waggles   Captain B. J. Hunnicut's (Mike Farrell) dog back home in the TV series M*A*S*H*.

White Flash   Tex Ritter's horse.

Whitey   White Owl Cigars' owl.

Willie   Kool cigarettes penguin.

Xantippe   Socrates' shrewish wife.

29

And Still More Names

IF you're still undecided, here is a potpourri of additional random names to choose from. And, if you still can't make up your mind, sleep on it for awhile. Tomorrow you can always reread *What to Name Your Dog*.

A
Action
Adieu
Aesop
Aladdin
Alfalfa
Alibi
Alimony
Aloha
Amazon
Amber
Amigo
Angel
Applejack
April
Aquarius
Aries
Arrow
Arson
Ayatollah

B
Baby
Badger
Baldie
Balmy
Bambi
Bamboo
Bandit
Bangs
Bangles
Banjo
Banner
Bantam
Baron
Barracuda
Barty
Bawdy
Beauty
Bengal
Biddy
Big Boy
Big Red
Bingo
Bittersweet
Blackberry
Blackfoot
Blackie

Blackjack
Blarney
Bleep
Blimp
Blinky
Blockhead
Blossom
Blot
Boggle
Bojangles
Bones
Bonkers
Bonnie
Boomer
Boots
Boss
Bourbon
Bow
Boy
Boyfriend
Braids
Brains
Brandy
Brass
Brat
Bratty
Brave
Breathless
Breezy
Briar
Brownie
Brutus
Bubbles
Buck
Buckets
Buckeye
Buckhorn
Buckwheat
Buff
Bull
Bullet
Bummer
Buns
Butch

Butterball
Buttercup
Butterfly
Buttons

C
Cactus
Calcutta
Camaro
Candy
Capers
Captain
Cashmere
Cavalier
Champ
Chap
Charlie
Charity
Chaser
Chastity
Checkers
Cheerio
Cheers
Cheerful
Cherry
Cheyenne
Chi-Chi
Chicory
Chipper
Chips
Chocolate
Choo-Choo
Chow
Chuck
Chug-a-lug
Cigarette
Cinnamon
Cisco
Clinker
Clipper
Clover
Clown
Cocoa
Coffee

Colby
Colonel
Colt
Comanche
Comet
Congo
Cookie
Corky
Cornstalk
Corny
Cosmos
Count
Cowslip
Crackerjack
Creep
Cricket
Crocus
Crunch
Crusader
Cuddles

D
Daddy-Kool
Daddy-O
Dakota
Damnit
Dancer
Dandy
Darling
Dart
Deacon
Demon
Devil
Dilly
Dimples
Ditto
Diva
Dolly
Domino
Doodles
Dotty
Dracula
Dragon
Dreamer

Dreamy
Duds
Duesenberg
Duke
Dynamite

E
Eager
Eagle
Easy
Ebony
Echo
Ego
Electra
Empire
Ergo
Ethics
Eureka
Express
Eyebrow

F
Faith
Falcon
Fame
Fancy
Fangs
Fast Food
Fatso
Fauntleroy
Fearless
Feathers
Feller
Ferrari
Ferry
Fickle
Fiddle
Firecracker
Fiver
Flag
Flake
Flame
Flapper
Flash

Flasher
Flim-flam
Flip
Flyer
Fluffy
Folly
Frankenstein
Franks
Fraülein
Freckles
Freebie
Freeway
Frenzy
Friday
Frizzle
Frizzy
Frosty
Fuddy-Duddy
Fudge
Funk
Funnyface

G
Gangbuster
Gardenia
Gemini
Geronimo
Gidget
Giggles
Gigolo
Ginger
Gingerbread
Girlfriend
Gourmet
Greaser
Greetings
Gretchen
Grouchy
Grunt
Gumbo
Gumby
Gunther
Guppy
Guy

H
Handy
Happy
Half-pint
Haywire
Hazelnut
Hibiscus
Highball
Highness
Hodgepodge
Hornet
Hot Lips
Hulk
Hunter
Hustler

I
Impy
Ink Spot
Inky
Ivory

J
Jackel
Jade
January
Jazz
Jemmy
Jet
Jiffy
Jigger
Jingles
Jinx
Joker
Jollies
Jolly
Jubilance
Juggernaut
Juice
Jumble

K
Kickapoo
Kicks

157

Killjoy
Kilroy
King
Kiss
Kisser
Kool

L
Lacey
Laddie
Leatherneck
LeBaron
Leftovers
Lex
Libra
Licorice
Lilac
Loafer
Lobo
Loco
Lord
Loveless
Lover
Lovesick
Lubber
Lucky
Lucky Lad
Lummox
Lustful

M
Mac
Maddy
Mademoiselle
Maestro
Magic
Magnet
Majesty
Major
Mallard
Mandrake
Marbles
Marigold
Marijuana

Marmaduke
Marquis
Masher
Meatball
Meggie
Melancholy
Mercedes
Mickey
Mim
Ming
Miracle
Mischief
Mishmash
Mistress
Moccasin
Mohawk
Monarch
Monsignor
Monster
Moon
Mooch
Mops
Muddy
Mumbles
Mums
Munchkin
Mustard
Mutter

N
Navajo
Nerf
Nightingale
Nightmare
Noggin
No-Show
Nova
Nugget
Nutmeg

O
Obscene
Oddball
Oddfellow

Off-Beat
Old Faithful
Old Soldier
Olive
Oliver
Omen
Once-over
Oops
Opus
Oreo
Ornery
Outcast

P
Paddles
Paddy
Pal
Palsy-Walsy
Pamper
Parader
Patches
Paws
Payola
Peanut
Penny
Pepper
Peppermint
Peppy
Pixie
Playboy
Pocahontas
Pointer
Poker
Poppy
Pranks
Preacher
Pretzel
Pride
Prince
Princess
Prosperity
Pucker
Pueblo
Puff

Pumpkin
Punch
Puns
Puny
Pushy
Puzzle

Q
Queen
Quick
Quackers

R
Raffles
Rags
Rap
Rascal
Raspberry
Rax
Razorback
Razzle
Red
Renegade
Rex
Ribbons
Riddles
Riff
Riffraff
Rinky
Rip-off
Robot
Rocket
Rod
Rogue
Rook
Rootsy
Rubles
Ruckus
Rudolph
Rumble
Rummy
Runner
Runt
Rusty

S
Sad Sack
Sandy
Sargeant
Sassafras
Sassy
Saucy
Savvy
Sawbuck
Scamp
Scarlet
Scrappy
Scorpio
Scout
Scruples
Scuff
Scuzzy
Senator
Shadow
Shameful
Shane
Shangri-La
Shawnee
Shenandoah
Sherry
Shimmy
Shindig
Shiny
Shoddy
Shoe
Sidekick
Silhouette
Silver
Simmy
Sinbad
Sioux
Sixpence
Sizzle
Skipper
Sleazy
Sleek
Sleeper
Sleuth
Slicker

Slowpoke
Slugger
Small Change
Small Fry
Small Job
Smarts
Smasher
Smoky
Smooch
Smoothie
Smutty
Sneakers
Snap
Sniff
Sniffle
Snoopy
Snowball
Snowflake
Snow White
Snuggles
Socks
Sombrero
Soppy
Soupy
Sorry
So-So
Soufflé
Southpaw
Spanky
Sparkle
Spearmint
Speedy
Spice
Spooner
Spot
Squeaker
Squire
Squirmy
Star
Stark
Stinky
Stud
Sucker
Sugar

Sugarfoot
Sundance
Sunshine
Superstar
Sweetheart
Sweetness
Sweet Potato
Swifty

T
Tacky
Tadpole
Taffy
Tag
Tall Job
Tammy
Tap Dance
Taps
Tasso
Tattoo
Taurus
Tecumseh
Tequila
Thumper
Thunder
Thunderbird
Tickles
Tidbit
Tiffany
Tiger
Tim
Tinker
Tinsel
Tiny
Tippy
Tom-Tom
Topper
Toto
Touché
Trapper
Trapps
Trifle
Trinity
Trinket

Trojan
Troubles
Tuffy
Tulips
Tumbleweed
Turn-on
Tutti-Frutti
Twiggy
Twinkle
Two Bits

U
Ugly
Ulcers
Unique
Urchin
Useless

V
Vampire
Vaseline
Velvet
Viking
Violet

W
Wailer
Wallflower
Warrior
Wasp
Welcome
Whip
Whiskers
Whiskey
Whisper
Whiz
Wichita
Wiggins
Willy
Wimp
Wimpy
Wincer
Winner
Woody

X Y Z
Xeno
Xerox
Xerxes
X-Ray
Yank
Yankee
Yelper
Yonkers
Yorkie
Zany
Zap
Zebra
Zelda
Zep
Zero
Zip
Zipper
Zodiac
Zorba
Zorro